Family Life in a Northern Thai Village

Sulamith Heins Potter

Family Life in a Northern Thai Village

A Study in the Structural Significance of Women

UNIVERSITY OF CALIFORNIA PRESS
BERKELEY · LOS ANGELES · LONDON

University of California Press
Berkeley and Los Angeles, California
University of California Press, Ltd.
London, England
Copyright © 1977 by
The Regents of the University of California
First Paperback Printing 1979
Second Cloth Printing 1979
ISBN 0-520-04044-9 paper
ISBN 0-520-03430-9 cloth
Library of Congress Catalog Card Number: 76-52035
Printed in the United States of America

5   6   7   8   9

To J. and E.

Contents

Illustrations

Maps:

Figure

Plates

Acknowledgments

I would like to thank the people of Chiangmai Village, especially Moonlight, Full of Fineness, and Holy Day, whose help and friendship I value greatly. I want to express my gratitude to Professor Burton Benedict, one of the finest teachers I have ever encountered, for his conscientious, constructive, and good-humored comments and criticisms; and to Professor William Simmons. I would like to thank my husband, Professor Jack M. Potter, most affectionately.

The fieldwork on which this research is based was supported by a grant from the National Institute of Mental Health.

The maps and plans in this book are the work of Adrienne Morgan.

I am grateful to Juree and Vicharat Vichit-Vadakan and Narujohn Iddhichiracharas for their kind help.

Cast of Characters

BLESSING Second daughter of Mother Celestial and Father Good, the oldest of their children living in the main house.

CELESTIAL Mother in the main house, she is daughter of Grandmother Worth and Grandfather Ten Thousand, and wife of Father Good.

CHARMER Oldest of the four daughters of Older Sister Clear and Older Brother Eye, she lives in the small house.

CLEAR Oldest daughter of Mother Celestial and Father Good, now married to Older Brother Eye, with four daughters of her own; her family lives in the small house.

EYE Son-in-law of Mother Celestial and Father Good, husband of Older Sister Clear, and father of the family in the small house.

FEMININITY Youngest of the four daughters of Older Sister Clear and Older Brother Eye.

FINE QUALITIES   The third daughter of Mother Celestial and Father Good; she died in childbirth.

GOOD   Husband of Mother Celestial, father of the family, and head of the main house.

HOLY DAY   The sixth daughter of Mother Celestial and Father Good; she suffers from a speech impediment.

KEEN   The only son of Mother Celestial and Father Good, their sixth child.

MOONLIGHT   The fourth daughter of Mother Celestial and Father Good, and the anthropologist's most important informant.

NEW DAWN   Youngest daughter of Mother Celestial and Father Good, she is most likely to inherit the main house.

PEARLY SMOOTH   Third of the four daughters of Older Sister Clear and Older Brother Eye, she lives in the small house.

RED   Second of the four daughters of Older Sister Clear and Older Brother Eye.

SPIN OUT GOLD   The fifth daughter of Mother Celestial and Father Good, born with a defect of the foot which makes her limp.

TEN THOUSAND   Late husband of Grandmother Worth, father of Mother Celestial.

WORTH   Widow of Grandfather Ten Thousand, mother of Mother Celestial, the senior woman through whom house and lineage membership have come.

The names are translated from Northern Thai names. The name of every individual mentioned in the text is a pseudonym, as is the name Chiangmai Village.

Where a word in Northern Thai has been transcribed rather than translated, I have used the orthographic system of Mary Haas (1967).

1

Theoretical Setting

In this book I am investigating the social structure and social organization of family life in a Northern Thai village. I am presenting my data in an essentially humanistic narrative form, because I believe that anthropology should be "history" in Alfred Kroeber's sense, or "thick description" in Clifford Geertz's. At the same time I hope to show the analytic shape which the data assume, and the theoretical importance of the analysis.

Specifically, it is my aim to describe a family system in which the significant blood ties are those between women—where the social structure is conceptually female-centered. Such a structure is importantly unlike structures in which the significant blood relationships involved are those between men; whether father and son, as in a patrilineal system, or mother's brother and sister's son, as in a matrilineal system. Where the relevant consanguineal ties are those between woman and woman, the logical consequence is that the structurally significant relationships between men are affinal. I shall discuss how this system differs from a male-centered system, and I shall examine its workings in a variety of social contexts.

I would argue that the assumption of the structural significance of men has made it more difficult for anthropologists to
grasp the structural principles of female-centered family systems; or at least the structural principles of the Northern Thai
system with which I am directly concerned, the structure of
which has for many years been described as "loose." The
system itself is not formless or inchoate, but its shape has been
difficult for anthropologists to see.

Since I am concerned with the anthropology of Thailand,
as well as with humanistic anthropological style and the theoretical implications of my analysis, it is important to place my
work in the context of previous anthropological research done
in Thailand. I begin in this first chapter by reviewing the relevant literature, and showing how my study is a departure from
it. Then I introduce the family I studied, as individuals who
form an integral social group, in the courtyard which symbolizes their social unity. I consider this family in terms of their
economic activities: as individuals vis-à-vis one another, as a
family group, and in relationship to other village families. I
then discuss the family members in relation to the village
temple. I explain the ordering of social relationships in the
family; I consider encounters with spirits, and what those
spirits imply about the social order of human beings; and con-
cluding comments follow.

My first task is to place this research in its scholarly context.
I have said that I am concerned with a classical anthropological question—the examination of the social structure and
social organization of family life. I am also concerned with the
impact of structure and organization on the experiences and
feelings of the people involved. Because of the paradoxical way
in which anthropological research in Thailand has developed,
the consideration of these classical questions is a relatively new
point of departure.

It was in Thailand that John Embree made the observations
which led to the formulation of his theory of loosely structured

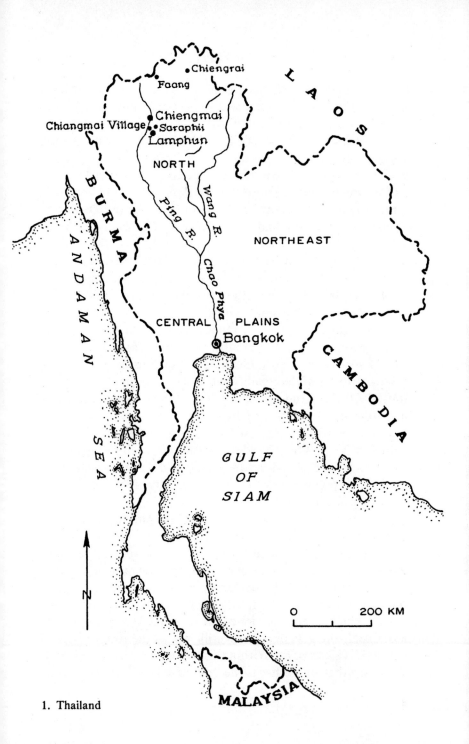

1. Thailand

social systems: social systems in which "the importance of observing reciprocal rights and duties" was minimized, with the result that "considerable variation of individual behavior was permitted" (1950, p. 4). As an integral part of his theory, Embree postulated a social system "relatively" lacking in social roles, and hence in forms of social structure and organization which would require the performance of role behavior. Anthropologists working in Thailand since the publication of Embree's ideas have had to take cognizance, whether admiring or critical, of his work, and until quite recently, anthropologists working in Thailand have been curiously reluctant to elucidate or explain Thai social structure, since Embree's theory implies that the attempt would prove fruitless. As Tambiah puts it, "Embree's formulation obstructs any kind of structural analysis . . ." (1966, p. 424). Although family and kinship relationships are the basic units of social structure in any society, and an understanding of kinship structure is essential to an understanding of social structure as a whole, until 1970 the structure of the Thai family received cursory attention in the published literature. In the last five years, however, increasing interest has been displayed in Thai kinship and family life. The ideas of Embree, so influential over the twenty-year period between 1950 and 1970, appear to be losing their potency now that a great variety of interesting new data have become available.

A brief summary of anthropological thinking about the Thai family and its structure, or lack thereof, will serve to put the results to be presented here into perspective. Embree himself is the first important figure to discuss the family. He says, ". . . The structure of the family is a loose one, and while obligations are recognized, they are not allowed to burden one unduly. Such as are sanctioned are observed freely [*sic*] by the individual—he acts of his own will, not as the result of social pressure" (1950, p. 6). Within this framework, Embree is willing to say that the father is the "putative head" of the family, but he does not describe the way a family works in any greater detail than that.

In 1953, Sharp et al. published *Siamese Rice Village, a Preliminary Study of Bang Chan*. In this book, which accepts Embree's theory of Thai society as a loosely structured system, the importance of the family is stressed, since "there are relatively so few groups to which the individual can belong" (1953, p. 77). Sharp describes the Thai family as consisting of parents and children living together in one household, and "thus very similar in its structure to the modern American family" (p. 77). According to Sharp, the Central Thai villagers of Bang Chan follow neolocal residence patterns. Husbands and wives are primarily obligated to each other and their children, rather than to their parents, and there is "no sense of lineage either on the father's or the mother's side" (p. 80). Property is divided equally among all children, with a slightly larger share to the child who stays to care for the parents in their old age. In many cases, the child who stays is the youngest daughter.

The next anthropological study, and the first based on field experience in the North, is John de Young's *Village Life in Modern Thailand* (1955). De Young recapitulates Embree's generalizations about the family. He says that "blood-relationship lines do not have the importance that they do in other areas of Southeast Asia" (p. 25). He adds an element to the composite picture of family life by observing that "the social position of Thai women is powerful" (p. 24), and he gives as evidence for this that it is women who control the money of the entire household. His comment is important because it foreshadows the emphasis on the importance of women in the social structure of the family which has become a focus of recent research, particularly my own.

Konrad Kingshill's book *Ku Daeng—The Red Tomb*, also based on fieldwork in Northern Thailand, appeared in 1960. Kingshill reports tendencies toward matrilocal residence and

5

village endogamy. In terms of relationships within the family, he says that "there is no trend toward patriarchy or matri- archy" (p. 51). In his opinion, "property rights within the family are similar to those recognized in Western society" (p. 53). Since Kingshill's primary interest is religious life, his data on the family are brief and sketchy.

In 1960, Howard Kaufman's *Bangkhuad: A Community Study in Thailand* was published, based on fieldwork in a Central Plains village. Kaufman gave more attention to the family than previous authors had done. He distinguished three kinds of family groups. His classification is based on where people live, but not on any normatively structural reason why they live there. The three kinds of family groups to which he refers are the household, the spatially extended family, and the remotely extended family. In describing his first category, the household, Kaufman says that it is run by the mother, who is the one who raises the children. He borrows Embree's phrase "putative head" to describe the father. He observed residence rules which require matrilocal residence for the first year of marriage, and patrilocal residence thereafter. As far as inheritance patterns are concerned, Kaufman says that the father controls the division of property, and that the rule is for each child to have an equal share of land, with the youngest son or daughter receiving the house and equipment. As for his second category, the spatially extended family, the mem- bers demonstrate relationship by helping one another in case of economic need. However, relatives are not required to ex- change labor—"there are no prescribed consanguineal obliga- tions concerning various aspects of the household economy . . . the modern Bangkhuad household does not depend on the extended family in agricultural matters, and the extended family does not form the economic unit" (p. 31). The members of Kaufman's third category, the remotely extended family, demonstrate relationship by contributing to funerals. The relationship between these social variables and Kaufman's locational typology seems arbitrary. Kaufman summarizes his findings in the light of Embree and his followers with the remark, "Some scholars have commented that the Thai have very little sense of family responsibility; but in Bangkhuad, responsibility toward one's family is by no means lacking" (p. 23). From the point of view of my findings on family structure, to be developed below, Kaufman's most interesting comment is one which he makes casually. In the course of a discussion of status and wealth differences between marriage partners, and a pressure against what he calls "too great a discrepancy" (p. 28) he recounts the following example: "A hamlet headman at Kilopaed has three unmarried daughters in their late twenties and early thirties. Only two men have dared to ask to marry them, and both were turned down by the father as being too irresponsible to be trusted with his property" (p. 28). The importance of this incident lies in the implication that authority over a family's property passes from father-in-law to son-in-law. Kaufman does not make this point, but it is crucial to my own argument, and repeatedly confirmed by my own data.

Herbert P. Phillips' *Thai Peasant Personality* was the next important addition to the literature, in 1965. This is an analysis of some psychological aspects of Thai social life, and the family is only discussed because of the bearing it has on personality. Phillips was very heavily influenced by Embree's theory of loose structure, and his research was done in Bang Chan, the Central Plains Village which had been studied by Sharp et al. Phillips' discussion is couched in terms of the way individuals feel about kinship, rather than in terms which describe the system in which the individuals are acting. He unifies the data he gets from individuals by considering the statistical patterns formed. He is not looking for what is shared, in a broad, normatively structural sense (in contrast with my attempts to understand the nature of the Northern Thai family system), but for what can be shown statistically

7

to be held in common. This means that his analysis is not a cultural one; or, to put it in Lévi-Strauss' terms, his model is statistical rather than mechanical (1953, p. 528). (I seek a mechanical model.) Phillips rejects the very existence of structural relationships in Thai kinship. He says, "Actually, I feel that any attempt to bring descriptive order to Bang Chan kinship does violence, in the very process of ordering, to the reality which is being described. . . . Kinship relationships in Bang Chan are considerably more unpredictable, inconsistent, and chaotic than our descriptive modes typically admit . . ." (p. 29). The only really structural phenomenon to which Phillips alludes is the set of respect relationships based on age within the family. He says, "The role of these respect patterns cannot be emphasized enough. . . . An older sibling['s] . . . position in the authority structure assumes the respect of those younger than he, and they willingly grant it, for, among other things, he plays his role well as the kindly superior . . ." (p. 33). These respect relationships apply to every member of the family, not merely to siblings. Phillips summarizes his views on the family by saying, ". . . It is not easy to determine the basis of the unity of the family. However, of all the factors which keep people living together in amity and affection, two come to the fore: a sense of love, obligation, and respect that is derived from the simple fact [one wonders what he means by this phrase] of kinship, but which must be continuously confirmed by mutual benefits; and economic considerations" (p. 32). This kind of explanation does not conceive of kinship as a cultural and structural form, and so does not elucidate its organization, working out, and peculiar qualities within a society. It carries the suppositions of the loose structure theory to their logical extreme.

Michael Moerman worked in a village in Northern Thailand, the inhabitants of which belong to an ethnic sub-group called the Lue. In 1966, Moerman tried another tack for understanding kinship in a loose-structure framework. He presupposed an essentially Westernized "biological" notion of kinship—perhaps this is what Phillips intends by his phrase "the simple fact of kinship"—rather than an anthropological model based on what relationship means to the people of the culture being studied. For Moerman, everyone in the village was kin, by his standards, so the basis of close ties had to be sought elsewhere. He says, "Ban Ping is a fairly small, predominantly endogamous community of bilaterally related kinsmen. Almost all of its 639 inhabitants have the same surname and can be traced back to fourteen ancestral couples. This means that every individual has more kinsmen than he can use. One simply cannot be especially intimate, especially supportive, especially helpful, to all of one's many relatives. In Ban Ping, and probably throughout Thailand, extragenealogical considerations are extremely important for determining whom one calls and behaves toward as 'kinsmen'" (p. 151). His paper attempts to trace some of these extragenealogical considerations, especially in the context of the village temple. His conclusion is of interest because he feels that the loose-structure theory is not, perhaps, as useful in understanding Thai society as had been consistently assumed and as he had presupposed himself; he says, "In the course of explicating the concept's meaning in Ban Ping, I have become less convinced of its value for depicting Thai society" (p. 167).

In 1967, Gehan Wijeyewardene's article, "Some Aspects of Rural Life in Thailand" attempted a kind of summary of what had been done so far. Wijeyewardene's fieldwork took place in a Northern Thai village near Chiengmai, which he calls South Village. He assumes, like Phillips, that structure in Thai society will have to be demonstrated by statistical models and analysis. He says, "In situations such as one finds in Thailand where there is an absence of clear-cut rules defining kinship ties and obligations, domestic structure can adequately be treated only through the use of statistical data" (p. 65). In the tradition of Embree, he remarks, "Thailand is well known for its absence of formal kin groups. . . . Does this mean that organization is alien to Thai culture?" (pp. 82–83). His discussion of what *is* known about Thai kinship and family organization is, as he himself says, "fragmentary and impressionistic" (p. 65). He feels that Kaufman's typology of family groups should be enlarged to include another category, the compound group. However, this new category is to be understood "not necessarily in land but in kin terms" (p. 66); this has the effect of further obfuscating the distinction between physical location and structural form, already blurred by Kaufman. Wijeyewardene says that, "There are no rules of endogamy or exogamy sufficiently rigid to act as important checks or stimuli to mobility" (p. 67). He describes residence as "bilateral with a tendency toward uxorilocality" (p. 69). He notices the existence of "personal and domestic spirits" (p. 74) inherited in the female line, but he describes them as "individual" spirits, and ignores the possibility that they may have significance in delimiting a kin group. He comments in passing on the importance of ties between male affines: ". . . Often ties between male affines could equal or exceed in importance ties between brothers" (p. 66). However, the focus of his attention is the weakness of fraternal ties, rather than the strength of affinal ones.

In 1968, the *Area Handbook for Thailand,* by Harvey Smith et al., was published by the U. S. Government Printing Office. This is a revision of an earlier work prepared by Wendell Blanchard as Chairman of the Washington branch of the Human Relations Area Files. It attempts to summarize all of the information currently available about Thailand. In discussing the family, the authors point to an emphasis on "individual independence and dignity [rather] than family solidarity" (p. 119). They describe the neolocal nuclear family as ideal, with men and women being regarded as equals, and children being obligated to defer to their elders. The authors indicate that family members are motivated by practical, economic sorts of considerations in acting or living together, rather than by a desire to conform to structural norms. They comment that in northern and northeastern villages, "kinship ties tend to become extremely complex" (p. 120), but they do not describe or analyze the complexity. (The authors are, in my opinion, unreliable with regard to Northern Thailand—perhaps because of the ethnic prejudices of Central Thai informants. They say, for example, "In the Northern Thai region, sexual liaisons may occur before marriage. Elsewhere, however, even the suggestion of physical intimacy is avoided . . ." [p. 124]. This is simply not the case. In Chiangmai Village, as I shall call my field site, there is a rigid standard of sexual morality.) The *Area Handbook* considers the question of residence rules, saying that where residence is not neolocal, it is more likely to be matrilocal than patrilocal. The authors feel that, "In rural areas, at least, fragmentation or dissolution of the family group is by no means uncommon" (p. 121), and they point to an emphasis on lateral rather than lineal kin. As far as a man's relationships with his affines are concerned, they say, ". . . During the time a newly married man resides with his wife's parents, he is considered to have obligations to them which take precedence over those to his own parents" (p. 123). Once again, no structural theme emerges from this summary; there is no clear pattern of ideals which order social action. The authors of the *Area Handbook* have compiled data without discerning shape or meaning.

In 1969, a volume called *Loosely Structured Social Systems: Thailand in Comparative Perspective,* under the editorship of Hans-Dieter Evers, attempted to review the loose-structure theory and the ways in which it has been used. Three of the authors collected in this book, Hans-Dieter Evers, J. A. Niels Mulder, and Steven Piker, make points about the Thai family which are of interest. Evers says, "Thais do not acknowledge any prescriptions regarding residence after marriage, living in extended family units, or cooperating in kinship groups"

(p. 120). But he also says, "If we order thirteen recently studied Southeast Asian villages according to the frequency of extended family households, at least two Thai villages including the famous Cornell village of Bang Chan, rank at the top of the scale. . . . In relation to other Southeast Asian peasant societies some Thai villages seem to have a relatively high proportion of corporate groups, namely extended family households" (p. 120). This suggests that there is a structural rationale for extended family households, but that the rationale has not been clearly sorted out and explained.

Mulder's article is important because he quotes an unpublished paper and personal communications from Jacques Amyot, otherwise unavailable to the scholarly community: according to Mulder, Amyot "found cooperating groups of in-laws as a structuring principle in the Northeastern Thai countryside" (p. 22). This is tantalizing information. Piker, on the other hand, says that ". . . the absence of corporate extended kin groups is a well-established feature of Thai society" (p. 62). Piker disagrees with Amyot's implication that there are lasting ties between affines in the context of economic cooperation. He says, "Economic cooperation, other than that occurring within the kindred, normally rests upon ad hoc dyadic ties and implies no lasting relationship between individuals and families. Enduring cooperative work groups, as such, are all but nonexistent" (p. 63). For Piker, the kindred "is not a corporate group whose existence normally transcends the lives of its members. It much more closely approximates a voluntary association . . ." (p. 64).

S. J. Tambiah's *Buddhism and the Spirit Cults in Northeast Thailand* (1970) was a new departure for several important reasons. First, he was neither daunted by the loose-structure theory nor seduced by statistical enticements, and second, he made an attempt to understand what was going on from a frankly structural perspective. Since Tambiah's analysis was being made for the purpose of understanding ritual behavior, he was concerned with defining what "the essential structural ideas bearing on ritual are":

> In short, there is in the village a tendency toward co-residence, in compounds, of married female siblings and classificatory phii-naung (matrilateral parallel cousins), owing to the custom of uxorilocal residence and the inheritance of residence rights in compounds by daughters rather than sons . . . the normal acting unit or grouping in the village is a 'household'. Co-residence in compound involves reciprocities between households in economic and ritual matters. . . . The essential structural ideas bearing on ritual are coded in terms of *principles of social classification* as portrayed by kinship terminology, rules of social distance symbolized in marriage rules, the ordering of generations, and the topology of social space embedded especially in the physical features of the house and compound.
>
> Although residence and inheritance patterns have a matrilateral colouring, kinship is bilateral and ego-oriented. . . . For most people, the number of kinsmen in the community, both cognatic and affinal, is . . . large. In fact, the entire village population consists of a social universe that is subject to a common scheme of social categorization *which contains or includes the particularities of ego-oriented reckoning within the generalities of the society or village-wide categorical scheme.* It is important to grasp this integrating principle (pp. 14–15). [In every case, the italics are Tambiah's.]

In this emphasis on the wide range of kin ties within the village, Tambiah's findings echo Moerman's. Another important feature of Tambiah's analysis is that it is diachronic, and attempts to trace a pattern of structural changes through time. He says that the cycle of compound structures is as follows:

1. . . . the parental household and households of married children, usually daughters;
2. when the parents die the link between sisters or more rarely between brothers and sisters will be the link between households;

3. in the next generation, classificatory siblingship (phii-naung) (especially matrilateral first cousinship) and more remote ties will link the constituent households (p. 14).

Tambiah is not interested in the social dynamics of households, taken one by one, nor in the effect of household structure and organization on individuals; however, his emphasis on the household as a religious unit points in an interesting direction, that of seeing how the social functions of the family in larger contexts, such as religious life, tend to influence its structure and organization.

Another study done in the Northeast was Koichi Mizuno's *Social System of Don Daeng Village* (1971). Mizuno summarizes his findings on kinship as follows: "Don Daeng Village is a bilateral society lacking any forms of unilineal organizations. There exist three varieties of kinship groups; families, multihousehold compounds, and kindreds, all of which are organized by bilateral principles with a strong emphasis on maternal kinsmen" (p. 83). In calling the system bilateral with emphasis on maternal kinsmen, Mizuno is taking a stand similar to Tambiah's; however, when he comes to discuss authority relationships in the family, his explanation is reminiscent of the earlier loose-structure approaches. He says, "There are certain limits to family responsibility and loyalty. The limits derive from the very nature of the family, which is not considered as an entity that exists indefinitely from past into future. [Perhaps this is an implicit reference to Mizuno's experience as a Japanese.] Authority within the family is restricted to a minimum and the family members seem to enjoy relative equality. The father is regarded as head of his family and the children are taught to respect their spouses at [*sic*] their parents. But the rules of conduct merely show what is proper and what is not; they are in no sense prescripts. The children decide on their own whether they will help with the farming or not. . . . As far as worldly life is concerned, there exists no idea of women as inferior to men" (p. 93). In this statement (which is greatly at variance with my own observations in Chiangmai Village) Mizuno seems to be trying to resolve the conflicting views of Tambiah and the followers of Embree, and at the same time interjecting his own evaluations founded on assumptions formed in Japan—not only assumptions about the ideological bases of family loyalty, but also about the status of women. The Thai differ explicitly with Mizuno's view on the latter point, and say so in the proverb which states that women are secondary to men in the same way that the back legs of the elephant are secondary to the front legs of the elephant. Mizuno says that in Don Daeng the "bilateral kindred . . . generally consists of all the descendants of the four grandparents and their siblings. The kindred is not a group in the strict sense, but simply a category of kinsmen who can be utilized for assistance . . ." (p. 100). He also says, "Villagers tend to feel that maternal kinsmen are more close than paternal kinsmen" (p. 104). And then, "Inclination to maternal side is observed in an old obsolete belief of *phy sya* . . . an ancestral spirit different from . . . the guardian spirits of the village. . . . The ancestral spirit is believed to take possession of small children and women. And the spirit is often that of the deceased maternal grandmother of the obsessed children or one of her deceased siblings. . . . Selfish and obstinate conducts [*sic*] or quarrels between siblings which might disturb family life offend ancestral spirits . . ." (p. 106). Mizuno emphasizes that this custom is dying out, and he does not see it as an element which delineates kinship structure. However, in three out of the four cases of spirit possession which he describes, the spirit is angry at a son-in-law, and punishes the child of that son-in-law. Mizuno does not make this point; he merely reports the data without analysis.

The appearance of Andrew Turton's article, "Matrilineal Descent Groups and Spirit Cults of the Thai-Yuan in Northern Thailand" (1972) marks a breakthrough in the understanding of the structural context of family life. He is not primarily concerned with family or household. He says that the village is divided into three levels of organization, "household, descent group, and local community" (p. 242). His interest is in the descent group. He finds "a system of matrilineal descent groups and associated cults" (p. 217), and notes his surprise at the discovery, since "they are not found elsewhere in Thailand, nor had they been reported by anthropologists who had worked in Northern Thailand" (p. 218). In fact, such cults were also independently discovered by Richard Davis, Jack Potter, and the present author, as well as Turton. Turton describes an ideal-type descent group model:

> The essential components of any group are ideally arranged as follows: there is a spirit lodged in a shrine which is located in a house site containing a house known as the 'original' or 'stem' house (*hyan kao*) in which lives a female member of the senior generation who is both ritual head and ritual officiant; focused on this person, spirit, and these structures is a localized group of matrilineally related households, a core of which is topographically contiguous, who say of themselves that they are 'of the same spirit' (*phii diaw kan*). . . . All people necessarily belong to one of these shallow matrilineages. Women are members by virtue of matrilineal descent and never belong to more than one group. . . . Male children are members of their mother's group by right of filiation. . . . The basic ideology is simple; at marriage a man buys entry into his wife's descent group. . . (pp. 220–221).

Turton is working in terms of structural norms; he uses statistical data illustratively. His emphasis on physical location and topology strikes me as unnecessarily heavy—in Chiangmai Village these locational ideals rarely occur in practice, but the social form which underlies the ideal is there without a doubt. Turton is concerned with the actions and behavior of men rather than women in the structural context he is describing, yet many of his points imply a crucial structural importance of women—an importance which he never explicitly recognizes, but which is inherent in his data. He deals briefly with some relationships within the family. He says, "At marriage a man's parents provide the small marriage costs; he then ideally works for his wife's parents for a substantial period. Thereafter a man's strategies may diverge from those of his parents. The man typically wishes to set up his own household; break and work his own fields; and acquire access to and liens on as much of his parents' *or* wife's parents' land as possible" (p. 240). In the context of a discussion of Buddhist ritual, Turton comments, "Interestingly a novice is said to make greater merit for his mother . . . it is not the father-son relationship which predominates" (p. 250). In the context of the ritual concerned with the ancestral spirits, "Within the groups, punishment is inflicted by spirits which have a matrilateral, possibly even female connotation. The interpretation of their action, gossip and innuendo apart, is controlled largely by men . . ." (p. 243). (This is not true of Chiangmai Village, where women are ritual interpreters of ancestral spirits.) He also says, ". . . The ritual position of the man is comparable to that of the woman in the traditional South East Chinese patrilineage, at least in the domestic cult of the ancestors . . ." (p. 221).

Turton raises the question of the role of descent groups in economic life, an issue with important potential implications for the understanding of the way the household functions in the social structure. However, he tries to deal with the economic importance of descent groups in historical terms: "it is appropriate to attempt an interpretation of the social function of the Thai-Yuan descent group by considering it in the context of ecological conditions and the social relations of production. This involves the invidious task of historical reconstruction . . ." (p. 228). The meaning of his data in terms of present day family life and social functioning remains unexplained. Turton does make the point that "the matrilineal descent group is not now a landowning corporation" (p. 230). He concludes by expressing his sense of "the absence of any conclusive evidence on the relation between descent groups and the economic system . . ." (p. 231).

The importance of Turton's contribution, then, lies in his recognition and description of the ancestral spirit groups, in the indications in his work which tend to show the structural importance of women in the Northern Thai social system— although these are merely indications and no more—and in his raising of the issue of the relationship between descent group membership and economic life, although this last issue is never resolved. His article is important for its suggestions.

Richard Davis, in "Tolerance and Intolerance of Ambiguity in Northern Thai Myth and Ritual" (1974), reaffirms Turton's observations, saying that the Northern Thai have "a form of ritual matriliny, and they are required to spend an initial period of residence at the home of the wife's parents" (p. 3). He says that "Northern Thai social structure . . . [is] dominated by female ties" (p. 9), but his analysis is in the male-centered mode of social thinking; he says, for example, "Any bits of arcane knowledge that women may possess are of such shabby quality that they can only be transmitted to other women" (p. 12). He also makes the baffling statement that mythology suggests ways of formally resolving "potential conflict between female affines" (p. 10). However, he gives no examples of such conflict, and since female affines tend to be separated by the residence rules and involved in different ritual cults, it is difficult to know what he is referring to. In Chiangmai Village the crucial structural conflicts tend to be between male affines. Davis makes perhaps his most important point in commenting that, "in spite of the structural dominance of women in northern Thailand, there is, as I shall show, an ideological dominance of men" (p. 11). He carries this point through in terms of a dualistic analysis based on opposition in myth and structure, but his points do not further elucidate kinship and family life.

This review of the literature is intended to give the reader a sense of the development of ideas about the Thai family over the last twenty-five years. There are clearly great differences in the observations of different anthropologists, and it is often hard to tell whether the differences are due to observed regional variation, or to theoretical bias. Anthropologists working in the Central Plains have consistently observed less structure than those who have worked in the North or Northeast, but the research which has taken place in the North and Northeast is also, by and large, the most recent, and the most remote from Embree's influence. In any case, several important elements have emerged from the literature, which, coupled with my own observations, form the basis for the explanation of Northern Thai kinship and family life which I am presenting here. Perhaps the most important element to emerge from the literature is the way in which kin group membership is symbolized by membership in the spirit cults. People of both sexes are born into the spirit cult of their mother, but a man is incorporated into his wife's cult group at marriage. Yet the higher status of men is symbolized at the same time by the wife taking her husband's family name at marriage. Another important element is the cultural expectation that marriage will be matrilocal, for a token period at least. This means that a married man is living with his wife's consanguines, who are his own affines. The important other men with whom he is likely to reside are his wife's father and brothers-in-law (Wi SiHu), all of whom have also married in. It is also important that inheritance rules divide property equally among all children, both male and female, with two corollaries: that the house should go to the youngest daughter, and that it is customary for men to sell out their rights to their sisters and brothers-in-law (SiHu).

All of these important elements are integral to my analysis. The Northern Thai family is ordered in a delicate and complex way. It is based on the dynamic interplay of two factors: the relationships between women which define the social structure and determine the important relationships between men, and the higher social status and formal authority of the men. Authority is passed from man to man, but by virtue of relationships to a line of women: it is passed affinally, from father-in-law to son-in-law. This system contrasts with both patriliny and matriliny. It is a sort of mirror image of patriliny, in which the important consanguineal links are between mother and daughter rather than father and son; there is indeed a sort of analogy between the position of the Northern Thai son-in-law and the Chinese daughter-in-law. However, the analogy cannot be pushed too far, because in the Northern Thai case authority belongs to the affine, and this alters the entire pattern. In matriliny, relationships between men through ties to women are important, but the ties to women are consanguineal, established at birth, not at marriage. (Incidentally, as far as I have been able to observe, the mother's brother is not of structural importance to a Northern Thai man.) In this system, it is not women who can be thought of as being passed around from consanguineal group to consanguineal group. Instead of "the blueprint of a mechanism which 'pumps' women out of their consanguineous families to redistribute them in affinal groups, the result of this process being to create new consanguineous groups . . ." (Lévi-Strauss, 1953, p. 546), I am describing a system in which the people who are redistributed in affinal groups are men. The structurally significant people are female, not male. I call this a female-centered system in contrast to patriliny and matriliny, which, as they are understood currently, would both be male-centered systems.

It is important to distinguish a social system which is female-centered, conceptually speaking, from a matrifocal social system. Matrifocality is "a type of family or household grouping in which the woman is dominant and plays the leading role psychologically" (Solien de Gonzales, 1965, p. 1544). In Northern Thailand the woman is not dominant, nor does she play the leading role psychologically. The system contrasts vividly with such matrifocal systems as the one in Java, for example, where matrifocality means "that the woman has more authority, influence, and responsibility than her husband, and at the same time receives more affection and loyalty. The concentration of both of these features on the female role leaves the male role relatively functionless in regard to the internal affairs of the nuclear family" (Hildred Geertz, 1961, pp. 78–79). In Chiangmai Village, the system is conceptually centered on women, but women are not more powerful or influential than men.

I want to show how this conceptually female-centered social system works from day to day, and what it implies for the feelings, emotions, and experiences of the people involved. In order to do this, I have taken a particular family as my example, so that the reader can see the richness and complexity of daily life and family relationships. This is a style of presentation, and does not mean that my research was limited to this particular family. Actually, I lived with two families in the village. The first family was recommended to my husband and me by the priest, when we asked at the temple where we might be able to stay. The father of the family turned out to be the priest's brother. We rented a room in his house, the room which had been used by the oldest daughter and her husband, and they moved across the lane into another house owned by the father. I began fieldwork, using a Northern Thai townswoman as a translator until I began to feel confident speaking Northern Thai myself. Living in this household, I became well acquainted with the family and with their closest friends and associates. I began the village census, and carried on intensive participant observation throughout the village.

One day I was visiting at the eastern end of the village, and I happened to call on the family, the Plenitudes, whom I later chose to be the example for this book. They were friendly and forthcoming, relatively speaking, and I felt that the rapport which developed between their daughter Moonlight and me was exceptionally good. We decided to see if we could build a small house of our own in the Plenitudes' courtyard, and this was arranged. After our move, intensive observation of this second family and their closest associates began. I also developed a good rapport with Full of Fineness, the daughter of the village head, and became well acquainted with her family. Full of Fineness made constructive comparisons between her own family and others in the village, and she used her own social ties to get intimate information on such delicate subjects as inheritance, which are not usually discussed. Full of Fineness, Moonlight, and Moonlight's sisters New Dawn and Holy Day worked for us as research assistants and also helped in the house. When we moved into town at the time our daughter Elizabeth was born, they came and lived with us, so that I could continue to work even when not physically present in the village. During this time we completed the translation of the census data, which gave detailed information about every household in the village. Later we returned with our baby daughter to our village house, and lived there for four more months.

My conclusions in this book, then, are based on participant observation in the classical manner, carried out for a period of a year, residence with two families and close relationships with others, extensive census data for every village household, and intensive interviews on family life with a wide variety of informants.

2

The Courtyard

Chiangmai Village in Northern Thailand lies, emerald green and fertile, between two rows of misty blue mountains which define the Chiengmai Valley. The Plenitude family lives in Chiangmai Village. Their house is high-raftered, of weathered brown wood, standing on stilts and decorated with hanging baskets of plants. The house is the focal point of a courtyard bounded by hedges and paved with hard packed terra-cotta colored earth. In front of the house is the well; behind the house are the high coconut palms, and on either side the lamjaj trees (*Euphoria Longana*), the fruits of which are the village's most important cash crop. The lamjaj trees are bare except for the tips of their branches, where coarse green leaves grow thick. Hens scratch, and chicks ebb and flow around them. Two dogs bark wildly at every visitor. The Plenitudes come and go in the courtyard. Nine of them live in the house, and they form the largest household in the village. They share the courtyard with another household, the household of the oldest Plenitude daughter. She lives in a small bamboo house, weathered and stained green where water drips down the walls, with her husband and four children. The courtyard is

1. Rice Fields of Chiangmai Village.

the symbolic setting of the social lives of these fifteen people,
an extended family made up of two households (see kinship
diagram). I have taken them as a cast of characters whose
experiences exemplify and explain what family life is in Northern Thailand, the particular form and structure of a family
in this culture, and the feelings and experiences which grow
out of a family life structured in this way.

The courtyard forms a large irregular rectangle (see plan 1).
On the east, the courtyard ends at an irrigation canal over-
grown with trees and shrubs. Beyond the canal are the rice
fields which lie between Chiangmai Village and the next

24

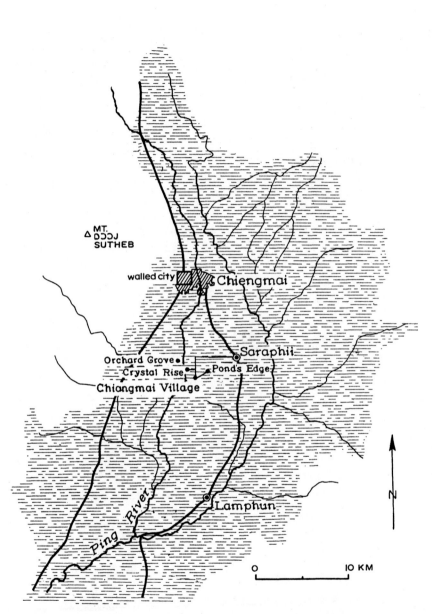

MT.
ᗨᗷᗷᒍ
SUTHEB

walled city

Chiengmai

Orchard Grove

Crystal Rise

Chiangmai Village

Saraphii

Pond's Edge

Lamphun

Ping River

N

0   10 KM

2. The Chiengmai Valley

25

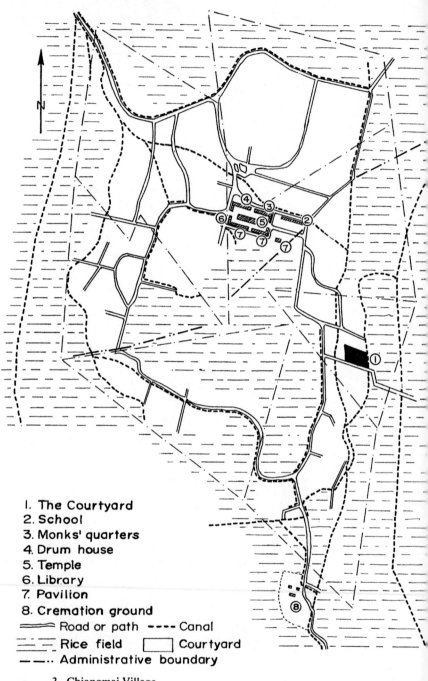

1. The Courtyard
2. School
3. Monks' quarters
4. Drum house
5. Temple
6. Library
7. Pavilion
8. Cremation ground
≋ Road or path ---- Canal
≡≡ Rice field ☐ Courtyard
—·· Administrative boundary

3. Chiangmai Village

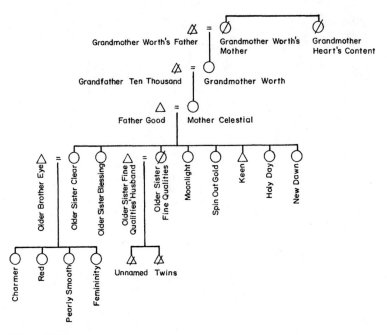

Kinship Diagram

village. On the south, a hedge runs the length of the court-yard, and beyond that is the lane. If you face north, the center of the village is down the lane to the left, and the rice fields east of the village are to the right. To the west, through a gap in the hedge, is another courtyard and another house. Beyond the Plenitude house on the north there is a hedge, a narrow footpath, and more houses. Other villagers live on two sides of the courtyard, then, north and west, the lane is to the south, and on the east are the open fields. The main house is at the west end of the courtyard, the small bamboo house at the east, and the house of the anthropologists is between them, in the center of the courtyard.

Casual visitors to the courtyard are entertained in the space under the main house, where a sitting platform and a bamboo

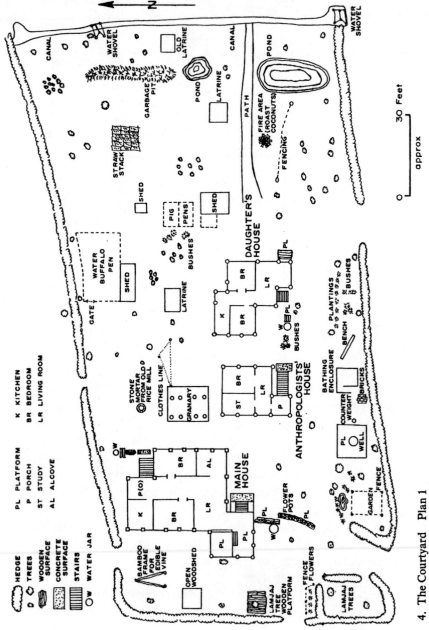

28

4. The Courtyard   Plan 1

LEGEND:
- HEDGE
- TREES
- WOODEN SURFACE
- CONCRETE SURFACE
- STAIRS
- W WATER JAR

- PL PLATFORM
- P PORCH
- ST STUDY
- AL ALCOVE

- K KITCHEN
- BR BEDROOM
- LR LIVING ROOM

30 Feet
approx

N

Labels on plan:
- CANAL
- WATER SHOVEL
- GARBAGE PIT
- OLD LATRINE
- POND
- LATRINE
- CANAL
- POND
- WATER SHOVEL
- FIRE AREA (ROAST COCONUTS)
- FENCING
- PATH
- STRAW STACK
- SHED
- PIG PENS
- SHED
- SHED
- WATER BUFFALO PEN
- SHED
- GATE
- BUSHES
- LATRINE
- DAUGHTER'S HOUSE
- BR
- LR
- K
- BR
- W PL
- BUSHES
- PLANTINGS
- BUSHES
- BENCH
- BATHING ENCLOSURE
- STONE MORTAR FROM OLD RICE MILL
- CLOTHES LINE
- GRANARY
- ST BR
- LR
- P
- ANTHROPOLOGISTS' HOUSE
- COUNTER WEIGHT
- PL
- WELL
- BRICKS
- W
- BR
- P(O)
- K
- BR
- AL
- LR
- MAIN HOUSE
- PL
- FLOWER POTS
- PL
- W
- PL
- GARDEN FENCE
- BAMBOO FRAME FOR EDIBLE VINE
- OPEN WOODSHED
- PL
- LAMJAI TREE WOODEN PLATFORM
- FENCE FLOWERS
- LAMJAI TREES

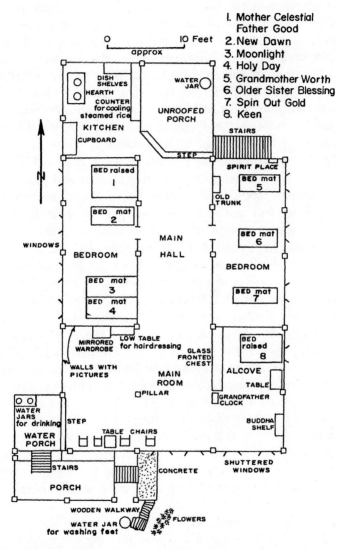

5. The Main House   Plan 2

bench have been set up among the square concrete pillars which support the building above. Visitors whose purposes require more formality are invited to come up and enter the house itself (see plan 2). The main house is dimly lit by the light from the barred windows. From the doorway at the top of the stairs, the main room in which visitors are entertained extends across the width of the house. The floor is beautifully polished. The walls are covered with snapshots and photographs, because the Plenitudes think it proper that every person and every event of importance to them as a family should be recorded. The present king and queen of Thailand and the two previous kings are given a prominent place. There are formal portraits of Mother Celestial and Father Good, the father and mother of the family. (The terms father and mother are used with the person's name to address or refer politely to any married person between the ages of fifty and sixty-five who has had children.) There is a portrait of Grandfather Ten Thousand (the terms grandfather and grandmother are used analogously), Mother Celestial's father, who died two years ago. He held the formal authority over the courtyard until his death. Under his guidance the family became powerful and important in the village, and Grandfather Ten Thousand was greatly respected by his fellow villagers. His funeral was an important ceremony in the family's history, and six or seven pictures of it are arranged along the wall in a series. There is a portrait of Grandmother Worth, Grandfather Ten Thousand's widow. Now she is old and difficult to communicate with, but at one time she was the peacemaker of the family, according to her grandchildren. She used to mediate between her husband who angered easily, and the other members of the family, all of whom were subordinate to his authority. A small picture, decorated with a paper flower, shows Older Sister Fine Qualities, who was the Plenitudes' third daughter. She died in childbirth while Grandfather Ten Thousand was still alive, a little over two years ago. Older Sister

2. Entrance to the main house.

3. Photographs, glass-fronted case, and the mirrored armoire.

4. Photographs—the top row, L to R, are Keen at his ordination, Mother Celestial, Father Good, Grandmother Worth, and Grandfather Ten Thousand.

Fine Qualities is important not only because the Plenitudes loved her while she was alive, but also because a death in childbirth is believed to result in an especially malevolent ghost, which might do the family harm. There are other pictures on the walls commemorating events which have been important to members of the family: Keen, the only son, with a farmers' youth group, and at his ordination as a novice in the monastery; Moonlight, the fourth daughter of the family, at her graduation from hairdressing school. (People of the same age or younger than one's self are addressed by their names alone. Since I am older than Keen and the same age as Moonlight, I refer to them here by their names without any other term of address.)

This picture-decorated main room is sparsely furnished. There is a sort of armoire with a full length mirror on the door and a dressing table built onto one side, which was made for Moonlight to seat her customers in front of, while she cut their

33

hair. This is to the left as one enters the room. Beside it along the wall are glass-fronted cases which lock. These cases contain embroidered pillows, souvenir dolls, and other valuables. To the visitor's right is a long wall which is really a row of windows. The windows are open to the breeze by day and shuttered at night. Ranged along the wall under the windows are four hard wooden chairs and a small table to match, covered with oilcloth. Straight ahead, at the far end of the room, is a shelf with a Buddha image displayed in front of a decorated mirror. To the left of that is an alcove where Keen, the only son, has his bed and a table. Sometimes Keen sleeps in his alcove during the day, heedless of visitors or family in the main room.

The rest of the house extends off to the left of the main room. There is a lofty central hall, above which the undersides of the pottery roofing tiles are visible. There are two long bedrooms, the same length as the hall, one to the right of a person

5. The Buddha shelf.

6. Chairs and table.

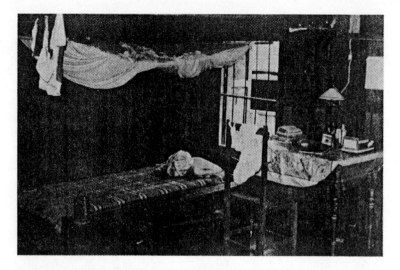

7. Keen's sleeping alcove.

facing down the hall, and the other to the left. In Chiangmai Village the most auspicious directions are east and north;[1] people sleep with their heads, the noblest parts of their bodies, to the east, and higher status people—or spirits—should be located to the north of lower status people. The members of the family have beds placed so that those who should receive the most respect have the positions to the north; the head of each bed is to the east. The extreme north end of the eastern bedroom is reserved for the spirits of the family's matrilineal ancestors.

The Plenitude family once consisted of Grandfather Ten Thousand, Grandmother Worth, Father Good, Mother Celestial, and eight children, seven girls and a boy. Now Mother Celestial's father, Grandfather Ten Thousand, is dead, the oldest daughter is married and lives with her husband in the little house, and the third daughter has died in childbirth,

1. Similar findings are reported by S. J. Tambiah, *Buddhism and the Spirit Cults in North-east Thailand* (1970). He says that "East is auspicious, represents life, is sacred. . . . West is inauspicious, represents death. . . . North is auspicious. . . . South is of neutral value" (p. 21).

8. The hearth, with baskets stored above.

which leaves nine. The oldest remaining family member, who should in theory receive the most respect is Grandmother Worth, who is Grandfather Ten Thousand's widow, the gentle and rambling old lady. She has her sleeping mat and mosquito net in the north end of the east room, next to the shrine for the spirits. This is the place she shared with her husband in the old days before he died. She has an ancient red lacquer box which she keeps at the foot of her bed for private valuables.

Next to Grandmother Worth, but separated from her by three or four feet of floor, sleeps Older Sister Blessing. Older Sister Blessing is the oldest daughter still at home. She is thirty-one, tall and plump, and continually tired. Older Sister Blessing is responsible and hardworking. She is still unmarried, and the best friends of her childhood have all died young. This has set her apart.

The south end of the long east bedroom is the place for Spin Out Gold's mat. She is the fifth of the original seven daughters, and probably the least loved by her mother, or so the other villagers say. Spin Out Gold was born with a defect of the foot which makes one heel too small. She limps under the heavy double baskets that she carries hanging from a balancing stick across her shoulder. Spin Out Gold is sociable, and loves to laugh, but avoids answering questions on serious subjects. She is engaged, but her parents do not like the marriage, because the boy is poor. Spin Out Gold is trying to earn enough money to leave home.

In the west bedroom, at the honorable north end, Father Good and Mother Celestial share a raised bed, the only raised bed, since the others sleep on mats. The knives of the household are tucked into the woven bamboo walls near the bed. Knives of all sorts—cleavers, machetes, small curved knives for cutting rice stalks—form an impressive array. Their mosquito net hangs in festoons from the ceiling. Father Good and Mother Celestial have been married for over thirty-six years.

They have lived their lives together under the domination of Grandfather Ten Thousand, Mother Celestial's father—a domination from which they are very lately released. Closest to their big bed is New Dawn's sleeping place. New Dawn is the youngest daughter. In theory, her bed should not be at the north end and people comment that she clings to babyhood by sleeping with her mother. She is a hard worker when she wants to be. Because she is the youngest, everyone else is entitled to give her directions and orders, and if she wants to be good and polite, she must do as they tell her. However,

9. Grandmother Worth.

10. Father Good.

11. Mother Celestial.

12. Older Sister Clear.

13. Older Sister Blessing.

14. Moonlight.

15. Spin Out Gold.

16. Keen.

17. Holy Day.

18. New Dawn.

New Dawn has developed techniques of passive resistance. Often she tells people that she will obey them in a minute, and then she extends the minute to many.

The bed next to New Dawn belongs to Moonlight. Moonlight was the fourth daughter, but since the death of Older Sister Fine Qualities she is the third—only Older Sister Blessing and Older Sister Clear, who lives next door, are older than she is. Moonlight is a complicated character, and one of my closest friends in the village. She likes to have things done properly, according to the ideals, but her affection for the ideal is usually thwarted by an imperfect reality. The other villagers sometimes say that she is "sŭuŋ," which means that she considers herself superior; she denies this, because it would not be proper of her to feel anything of the kind, but it is probably true. Moonlight is twenty-eight, and her chances of marrying are no longer very great. She is bright and competent herself, but intolerant of the failings of others.

The last bed, at the far south end of the west room, belongs to Holy Day. Holy Day is older than New Dawn but younger than all the others. She is very delicate and little. She has suffered from birth from an impediment to speech which the people of Chiangmai Village describe as the absence of a small second tongue in her throat. When she talks she sounds muffled and honking. She is smaller and slighter than any of the others. When she feels shy, she avoids speaking altogether, but when she does speak, what she has to say is usually straightforward. The other Plenitudes tend to be elliptical and evasive by comparison. Holy Day seems the most easily hurt, or perhaps the least adept at concealing pain. She is gentle and vulnerable. These, then, are the bedrooms with the beds and sleepers in order.

The Plenitudes' kitchen is beyond the west bedroom. The central hall extends onto an open porch; steps down are on the right of this, and the kitchen is on the left. It is Mother Celestial's domain. She loves food and eating. The kitchen is blackened from the cooking fires, which are made in two small potlike braziers on a hearth. Over the hearth is a frame which lets down from the ceiling on ropes. The frame is piled high with baskets, which are stored over the fire because smoke protects them from insects. The kitchen is furnished with a screened cupboard which is used to store dishes and leftover food, and a long narrow wooden table which holds the equipment for steaming and storing glutinous rice—a straight-sided wooden pot for steaming, and special baskets with lids for storing. Glutinous rice is soaked overnight, cooked in the morning, and eaten cold out of the storage baskets. It is eaten with a variety of curries and stir-fried vegetables, most of which require long preparation of ingredients but short cooking time. The preparation of ingredients is done by all the daughters, but especially Older Sister Blessing and Moonlight (directed by their mother) on the back porch which adjoins the kitchen. The back porch is open to the breeze and the sky. Food is chopped here on a board made from a round slice of a tamarind tree. The women pound spices with a mortar and pestle and put rice to soak in a beautiful green celadon jar. Fish caught in the streams and irrigation canals are brought back alive and swim in a dilapidated metal pot nearby. Sometimes friends gather on the porch to help make special food—sweets made from rice and coconut and steamed in banana leaves to donate to the temple, or chopped meat for the housewarming ceremony of a friend.

A wooden stair-ladder leads down from the porch to the courtyard below. The courtyard is where the animals live: flocks of little chickens, Holy Day's ducks, which are trained to forage by themselves in the fields every morning and come back by themselves at night, the two big dogs and a lame puppy, a marmalade colored cat, and, in pens, two pigs and a water buffalo.

There are three more buildings in the courtyard; a rice granary, which is like a one-room house on stilts with a miniature veranda around it, the anthropologists' house next to the granary in the center of the courtyard, and the small bamboo house belonging to Older Sister Clear, her husband, and her four young daughters. Older Sister Clear is a professional market woman, which forces her to keep very long hours; the market starts early and the preparation of goods for the next day goes on late. She is plump, pleasant, and careworn, because her family, whose labor is controlled and whose lives are dominated by her father, has a hard time making ends meet. Her husband, Older Brother Eye, is good-looking but very silent. An avoidance taboo prevents him from having anything to say to or do with his parents-in-law, who are always around. Older Sister Clear and Older Brother Eye have four daughters who range in age from eight to fifteen. The oldest is Charmer, a cheerful girl who is just beginning to be courted. Charmer has three younger sisters, Red, Pearly Smooth, and Femininity. Red is fourteen, gawky, and shy. She is sober where Charmer is bubbly. Pearly Smooth and Femininity are still in school: they are eight and seven respectively, and Chiangmai Village children stay in school until they are twelve. Pearly Smooth and Femininity wear white uniform blouses and blue skirts, instead of the flowered prints worn by older women. They are much less circumspect in their behavior than the adults. Sometimes they fight, and Pearly Smooth cries. Her sobs can be heard through the woven bamboo walls of the little house. In the afternoons, when school is out, the two play games together in the courtyard; a form of jacks in which small stones are caught on the back of the hand is very popular.

The social life of the courtyard includes some regular visitors. Foremost among these is Bright Eyes, aged fourteen months. Bright Eyes is the granddaughter of the family which lives next door to the west. All of the Plenitudes are fond of her, although she seems to like Older Sister Blessing best. Everyone encourages Bright Eyes to make the formal gesture of respect, palms together and fingers pointing up, and to say the polite words of greeting. Bright Eyes has been asked to do this so often that she only obliges if she happens to be in the mood. Her cousin, a gentle boy of twelve, usually comes with her and takes her home when she gets tired. Another regular visitor is Older Sister Valuable, who lives across the lane to the south. She is in her forties, with one son, but lives with her mother because her husband left her many years ago. In fact, he left another woman to marry her, and then left her when she became pregnant and went back to his first wife. Older Sister Valuable, who says she doesn't want to have any more to do with deceptive men, is very alert and lively, with a sense of humor and a hot temper. Another regular visitor is Grandmother Heart's Content, who also lives across the lane. She is an old lady, matrilineally related to the Plenitudes and hence under the guardianship of the same protective spirits. She has a "tender soul," as the villagers call a personality susceptible to spirit possession. Once she was possessed by a spirit at a village spirit dance, and she danced for hours, shouting rudely at the spectators. But as a general rule she is very pleasant and sympathetic.

Salespeople come through the courtyard almost every day, buying livestock and selling pottery, mortars, baskets, or meat. Occasionally someone comes begging for rice, which is always given.

This courtyard is the setting and these people the cast of characters who play out the forms of the family life which I propose to explain.

3

Economic Life

Compared with the other villagers in Chiangmai Village, the Plenitudes are prosperous. In a village where a third of the households are landless and the average holding is 1.4 acres of rice land, the Plenitudes own 4.7 acres, and control the right to rent two more. This is very important among people who value nothing more highly than rice fields. The main source of cash income in Chiangmai Village is the delicate and exotic lamjaj fruit, which grows best in northern Thailand and finds a good market in Bangkok. In Chiangmai Village the Plenitudes have fifteen good lamjaj trees, an average number, but the trees bear well. Then they have another orchard in Teakwood Crest, Father Good's native village. The average household in Chiangmai Village has 4.3 members. With nine people in the household, the Plenitude family's economic efforts are not hobbled by lack of labor, and the labor of a family member who finds a paying job can usually be spared. In the context of the village the Plenitudes' position is comfortable and their status is high.

Rice land is the single most important factor in the Plenitudes' prosperity. The family's holdings have been consolidated over several generations, partly by luck, because inheritance by only children made division of the property unnecessary, and partly because of hard work and thrift. Father Good and Mother Celestial can trace the history of their present holdings as far back as Grandmother Worth's mother. Grandmother Worth's mother lived in a house on the site of the present courtyard with three other people: Grandmother Worth's father, Grandmother Worth herself, and Grandmother Worth's old maid aunt (MoSi) named Grandmother Crystal. (Before she became a grandmother, Grandmother Worth would not have been addressed that way, but it is simpler to refer to everybody consistently as he or she is referred to now.) When Grandmother Worth's parents died, they left all their land to Grandmother Worth since she was their only child. This legacy consisted of .4 acre of courtyard land, with fruit trees and the house, and 2 acres of rice land. Grandmother Crystal still lived with Grandmother Worth and the household consisted of aunt and niece (MoSi and SiDa). Then Grandmother Worth married Grandfather Ten Thousand, and he joined the household. At the time of his marriage Grandfather Ten Thousand sold out his interest in his parents' estate, which was located in the village of Four Cornered Pond. In time, he and Grandmother Worth used this money and some more that they had saved to buy 1.4 acres of rice land in Chiangmai Village, so that their holdings consisted of .4 acres of courtyard land and 3.4 acres of rice land. Of the five children born to Grandmother Worth and Grandfather Ten Thousand, only Mother Celestial survived infancy. The household consisted of four people again, Grandmother Worth, Grandfather Ten Thousand, Mother Celestial, and Grandmother Crystal. When Grandmother Crystal died of old age, she left her .4 acres of courtyard land and 1.3 acres of rice land to Mother Celestial. Then Mother Celestial married Father Good. His share of his parents' estate consisted of .3 acres of courtyard land planted with lamjaj trees, located in his native village of Teakwood Crest, and the right to lease 2 acres

53

of rice land in Chiangmai Village. (This land belongs to an old friend of Father Good's, a man who is the son of a close friend of Father Good's father.) The Plenitudes pay for the use of the land in shares of the harvest, but their right to lease it is not questioned. This is a valuable right in a land-hungry village. Now that Grandfather Ten Thousand is dead and Grandmother Worth has effectively passed on the property, Father Good and Mother Celestial own in all 4.7 acres of rice land, 1.1 acres of courtyard land, and the right to lease 2 acres of rice land.

The Plenitudes' estate will not survive the present generation. The custom is for property to be divided equally among all children, except that the house is given to the youngest daughter, who is expected to stay with her parents and care for them in their old age. When the Plenitudes' land is divided seven ways, each portion will be meager. The house should in theory go to New Dawn, but all the unmarried daughters could legitimately claim that they have stayed on to care for their parents. The Plenitude children rarely discuss inheritance; it is a subject fraught with tension.

The Family's Rice Growing Enterprise

Just as rice land is the most important kind of land, rice growing is the most important kind of work in the village. People feel that nothing is more comfortable than eating rice, and nothing more satisfying than a full granary, which is the only real security a village family can have. The cycle of the year revolves around the seasons of the rice crop. Father Good is the director of the Plenitude family's rice growing enterprise. He controls the labor of the six children living at home, and his authority extends to the family of Older Sister Clear and Older Brother Eye in the little house. Older Brother Eye, Charmer, and Red help with the Plenitudes' fields before they work on their own rented land. When the work day begins at dawn they come to Father Good for directions. The structural dominance of the father-in-law over the household of the son-in-law is the rule in Chiangmai Village, an integral part of the system according to which authority is inherited affinally. That is how it used to be between Father Good and his father-in-law, Grandfather Ten Thousand. Father Good wants to keep control over Older Brother Eye, while Older Brother Eye hopes to strengthen his position and minimize his father-in-law's domination. However, Older Brother Eye owes many important things to his father-in-law and could not manage without him. For example, the land Older Brother Eye rents belongs to one of Father Good's closest friends, and without Father Good's influence it might well be rented to someone else. The relationship between father-in-law and son-in-law is tense, and there is an avoidance taboo which prevents a son-in-law from dealing directly with his parents-in-law. If Older Brother Eye wants anything from Father Good or Mother Celestial, like the loan of a scythe or a basket or a lantern, he asks his daughters Charmer or Red to act as intermediaries and make the request for him. A son-in-law's position is a difficult one, and by custom Father Good is in a position of substantial power.

In Chiangmai Village, people start the rice crop as the rains begin in late May or early June. They scatter the rice seed in small nursery plots, and transplant the seedlings to larger fields later, rather than broadcasting the seed directly on the large fields as is done in some other parts of Thailand. The Plenitudes begin by preparing the fields: they take off the weeds and burn them, build up the dykes between fields, so that each field will hold water, let in the water, and plow, harrow, and puddle the mud with bare feet to smooth out lumps and push any remaining weeds under. Then they scatter the soaked and sprouted seed in the nursery field. When the seedlings have grown to a height of about a foot, the family transplants them. Then the fields of transplanted rice are kept wet and weeded until harvest time, when the rice is cut, threshed by beating into huge baskets, and carried home. Except for plowing, when the Plenitudes hire help, and the major jobs of transplanting and harvesting for which they exchange labor, all the work is done by the family. Some anthropologists working in Thailand have stated that there is very little formal sexual division of labor in Thai social life. Sharp, for example, says,

> In Bang Chan there are very few adult cultural roles, apart from those associated with religion, which can not be played by either men or women. Two of the most striking instances, in comparison with all other known cultures, is that women may do plowing and men may be "midwives". . . . Apart from strictly biologically determined activities, there are few rights, obligations, or actions which are associated exclusively with one sex or the other (1953, p. 88).

Kaufman modifies this position, saying, "Although there is an accepted pattern for the division of labor, it is by no means rigid" (1960, p. 21). Both Sharp and Kaufman seem to conceive of social norms as essentially inviolable, a position which seems unnecessarily extreme to me. In any case, Sharp's statement is not true in Chiangmai Village, where the villagers have a clear idea of which jobs are to be performed by members of each sex; when exceptions are made, they are remembered and commented upon. Moonlight tried plowing once; she is the only woman among her set of friends to have done so, and she says it was very difficult work, requiring a knack, that only a man could do that.

Since the jobs involved in rice growing are assigned by custom to men or to women, Keen as an only son tends to have a heavier work load than the daughters, who help one another with the women's part. Keen has to build up the dykes, do any plowing that the family has not contracted for, and harrow when the plowing is done, since all of these jobs are men's work, and Father Good no longer works in the fields. In former days, when Keen was too little to work in the fields and Father Good was no longer vigorous enough to do all the work alone, Moonlight violated the norms for the sexual division of labor and worked with her father to build up the dykes. She speaks of it as a special thing, a sacrifice on her part beyond the ordinary requirements of custom. Now that Keen is old enough to do the work himself she no longer does men's work. A woman could do most men's jobs when necessary, but the job of scattering the rice in the nursery plot is of particular ritual importance: the norms for the sexual division of labor can *not* be violated, and a man must do the work or the rice crop may suffer. Keen scatters the Plenitudes' rice seed. It is a job which takes skill, and the rice grains fall around him in even, semi-circular sprays as he works.

Like other agricultural work, the major jobs, transplanting and harvesting, for which labor is exchanged, are clearly divided into men's and women's tasks. Men are supposed to pull the rice seedlings and women are supposed to bind them into bunches; men carry them to the fields, while the women plant them; then, when all the bunches have been carried, the men join in the planting, but they plant with a different twist of the wrist, so that the distinction between men's and women's work is maintained by a conscious difference in style. (This is almost a way of embroidering on the patterns of the sexual division of labor.) At harvest time, women cut the rice, and men thresh it by beating the bunches into the giant rice-threshing baskets. Women carry it home, using double baskets suspended in balance from a bamboo shoulder stick.

The work of rice growing shapes a village family's life. At the busiest times of year, families pass down the lane in front of the Plenitudes' courtyard before dawn, their faces illuminated in the darkness by the yellow glow of the lamps they carry. The Plenitudes hear them go by and begin to stir. As the sun rises they all dress in long-sleeved shirts, so they will be protected from the ferocity of the sun, wrap long bandage-like strips of cloth around their legs to keep off the leeches which live in the flooded fields, and put on hats and wrap scarves to cover their necks. When everyone has dressed and eaten, they take their water jar, made of brown pottery with a long neck like a vase, and their transistor radio. They walk in single file along the narrow dykes to their fields as the sun begins to beat down. In the rice fields the heat is merciless. The sun blazes, and the water in the fields, warm as a hot bath, reflects the light up, so that there is a double glare. The work goes on all day, with a break for lunch and a brief rest, and then back to the fields. In the evening the workers go slowly home as the reflections in the flooded fields around them turn mauve. The conscientious Older Sister Blessing comes last of all, so tired that she can barely speak. The work of the fields is part of a villager's identity. Of a child who has left the village and taken up town ways, the people of Chiang-mai Village say, "He has forgotten the fields, forgotten the rice land."

For the heaviest jobs, where a great deal of work must be done under pressure of time, the people of Chiangmai Village form groups to help each other out. The ideal of helping one another, which the villagers call "cûaj kan," is very important in the village, both in morality and in practice. The priest preaches mutual cooperation in the temple, and parents urge it upon their children. No one should be left to work alone, if there is anyone to help. But cooperation is not indiscriminate. People remember carefully who helped them, and return the help they received on a day-for-day basis: they describe this with the phrase "ʔaw wan, tɔɔb wan," which means, "take a day, return a day." One day of an adult's labor must be returned with one day of an adult's labor. Any adult in a family may be sent to do the work. People help those who are most important to them first. As a general rule, villagers take particular care to help members of their immediate bilateral kin group, households which share the same matrilineal protective spirits, near neighbors, and political allies.

Every year the Plenitudes have help from twenty-six other village households, which send representatives when the family transplants the seedlings from the nursery to the larger fields, and when it is time to bring the harvest in. All of the twenty-six households have close ties to the Plenitudes, and have for years. For example, Father Seeker is one of Father Good's closest friends. His house is just across the hedge which bounds the Plenitudes' courtyard on the north, so they are near neighbors. The fields which Older Brother Eye rents belong to Father Seeker. The wife of Father Seeker is descended from a sister of Grandmother Worth's mother, so that the two families share the same matrilineal protective spirits. Father Seeker is assistant headman of the southern half of the village. Father Good, who sits on the school committee, participates actively in village politics too; the two are political allies. The Plenitudes also exchange labor with the household of Father Come, headman of the south half of the village. His house is four or five courtyards away, and his wife is not related to Mother Celestial, so that the matrilineal spirits protecting the two families are not the same. Nor are the two families related bilaterally. But Father Come and Father Good are political allies, and like to exchange labor to ratify and reinforce their relationship, so there is always a representative from Father Come's house among the people exchanging labor with the Plenitudes. Clearly the family's ties with some of the households which help them are stronger than with others. Nonetheless, the twenty-six households with which they exchange labor represent the most important ties the Plenitudes have, ties which are clearly more important than those with the other 181 households in the village.

When the representatives of all the twenty-six households which exchange labor with the Plenitudes gather together for an agricultural task they form a group of a special kind. The group is more than a set of simultaneous dyadic relationships. All the members share a responsibility to Father Good and meet year after year to fulfill it. They are proud that the group is large, and they know who should be present and the reason for any absence. However, they do not form a corporate group, since they lack an independent legal existence, property in common, or internal organization. The exchange labor group in Chiangmai Village is an intermediate social form, falling between the dyadic contract and the corporate group, in which all of the members recognize one another's membership and act together, but only for one specific purpose. Many of the households which exchange labor with Father Good exchange with one another, so that the same people meet together in group after group, the exact membership of each group differing depending on the household being helped. There is a core of households in the Plenitudes' part of the village which tend to exchange labor mostly with one another, but some of the core families exchange labor with a father-in-law's household, or a daughter's household, or a household with the same matrilineal spirits, which has no ties with any of their other exchange partners.

Father Good keeps a very careful mental record of each person who comes to help. When the households of these people transplant or harvest, he decides which of his children should go to help them, and for how long, so that the labor exchange will come close to balancing correctly, day for day. He must consider his own needs and the needs of the other households, so that he never accepts more than he can repay. The system of mutual obligation is delicate, complicated and of the highest importance.

Individual Enterprises

As long as the rice-growing season lasts, the Plenitude children are obligated to work under Father Good's direction, but when the work in the rice fields is finished, they are free for enterprises of their own. The young Plenitudes are responsible for buying almost every necessity beyond food and shelter out of money they make themselves. Money for clothing, entertainment, excursions, gifts to friends, instruction, and equipment must be earned, from the time that a child reaches the age of ten or eleven. All of the Plenitude children have money-making enterprises under way. A proportion of the profits from every enterprise is supposed to be given to Father Good and Mother Celestial, as a gesture of respect, to increase their comforts. Father Good and Mother Celestial have the reputation of being fond of money, and eager to accumulate and save as much as they can. This puts the children in a difficult position, between the desire to gain the reward of their parents' approval, and the necessity of securing their own comforts, both present and future, by keeping what they earn. New Dawn's friend Full of Fineness, who is the daughter of Father Come, the village headman, says that the Plenitude children are in an unusually difficult position. In Full of Fineness' family, the children turn everything they earn over to their parents, but they are not expected to pay for their own clothes and other expenses, and Full of Fineness' parents often give gifts to their children. Sometimes the gifts are valuable ones, such as gold necklaces. Full of Fineness says, "We know that they will give us back as much as we gave them." In the Plenitudes' household, the children are reluctant to turn much money over to their parents, because their own expenses are likely to be heavy, and their contributions are not balanced by gifts and favors, yet they feel badly because it is not really good behavior to withhold money from a parent.

The Plenitude children react differently to this situation, depending both on their characters and on their future prospects. Within the structure of the family Older Sister Blessing, the oldest unmarried daughter, seems to feel the greatest sense of responsibility to her parents and to the family as a whole. During the rice-growing season, she goes to the fields first in the morning, and comes home the last, hot and slow-footed, when all the others have already bathed, and are sitting around the courtyard, cool and refreshed. She is the hardest working and most conscientious. When the rice-growing time is past, she often earns money selling fruit in the market, but she turns most of her earnings over to her parents or spends them on family concerns, like hiring labor when the rice season comes around again. She has few clothes, and rarely takes the holiday excursions which are one of the villagers' favorite pleasures. Older Sister Blessing is not saving money for a future life in a household of her own, since she is thirty-one, and an old maid. Older Sister Blessing recently turned down a proposal from an older man with children, a widower, and says she never thinks about those things any more. Older Sister Blessing is an economic pillar of the Plenitude family.

By comparison, Keen's temperament and probable future within the structure of village family life make him something of a weak reed. He is looking for a wife, and it is customary for a man to leave his home and move in with his wife's family. (Matrilocal residence is explicitly the ideal; it occurs in 73 percent of all marriages in the village.) He will be part of another household, and any investment he makes in his natal family will be lost to him. He enjoys having new clothes and a motorcycle, so his personal expenses are high. There are advantages to remaining unmarried, since Keen avoids being subject to the authority of a father-in-law as long as he remains single. His actions appear indefinite and indecisive, because the structure of family life pulls him in two different directions.

The youngest sister, New Dawn, is in a position diametrically opposed to Keen's. She still feels emotionally dependent on her parents to a greater extent than her siblings do. She has her bed next to her mother, and as Older Sister Valuable across the way puts it, "She is still drinking her mother's milk." The inheritance customs of the village favor New Dawn because the youngest daughter is usually the one who gets the house. When New Dawn earns money, she gives all of it to Father Good. Pleasing her parents means more to her, and she knows she has an important stake in the family's financial future.

Moonlight, Holy Day, and Spin Out Gold are in a much more difficult position. They know that if they marry, their parents will not be able to afford to help them very much, and they will probably have to break the preferred residence pattern by moving to their husbands' houses, since, as Grandmother Worth says, "There certainly isn't any more room here." Moonlight still hopes to marry. Any money she gives to her parents will give her little beyond the satisfaction of having behaved properly. Up to a point, behaving properly means a lot to Moonlight, who is a person of strong ideals, but she is also proud. She has a high regard for money and prestige, and finds it almost unbearable to lose face. When Moonlight earns money, she wants to save it for her own future: she would like to be able to pay the tuition at a dressmaking school and buy herself a sewing machine. In the short run, she likes to spend money on things that other people will admire and envy, like her new silver watch. When she is in a cool, idealistic mood, she thinks of family loyalty and cooperation, but in the heat of anger she says, "After all, you have to think of yourself first." She is competent and ambitious, and these qualities put her into conflict with her own sense of the proprieties.

Spin Out Gold, like Moonlight, is caught between the household's interests, as represented by Father Good and Mother Celestial, and her own, but she has already made a clear choice. Spin Out Gold is engaged to marry a young man from a poor family. She is saving money for their household together. Spin Out Gold and her future husband do not plan to stay with the Plenitudes, except for a token period of initial matrilocal residence, but to live with his parents. This is not simply because of the lack of room. Mother Celestial and Father Good object to the young man, because they say he is too poor, and they almost succeeded in breaking off the engagement. Spin Out Gold is little motivated to give money to her parents. She will marry and then move out as soon as she can. Although she suffers from their demands and reproaches, she does not suffer so much from an internal conflict like Moonlight's.

A gentle, sweet-natured person like Holy Day feels these same pressures differently. Holy Day is young enough that she may well marry, unless her speech defect is regarded as an insuperable objection, and she is not so old that her desire for independence has stiffened her spine. She is sympathetic and really rather generous. When Holy Day makes money, she gives some to her parents, and some to Grandmother Worth, who tends to be neglected, before taking the rest.

There are a wide variety of ways to earn money, and the Plenitudes have tried most of them. They can grow peanuts, garlic, or soybeans during the season when the rice is not standing in the fields, or they can raise chickens, ducks, and pigs. There is temporary work picking lamjajs or planting someone else's garlic. Moonlight set herself up as a hairdresser, and Keen got a job on a construction project at the University of Chiengmai. The daughters have tried being market women, either on a small scale close to home, or on a grander scale in town. Each year, with reasonable luck, they can make enough to buy the things they need.

Holy Day has been raising peanuts with some success. She had to have some savings to start with, because she rented the field she used, and she had to hire a man to plow it, as well as buying the peanuts for seed. (The rental of the field for the season cost 25 ฿—the unit of money is the baht, worth five cents in 1972—so this was equivalent to $1.25, the plowing was 19Ƀ, or $.95, and the shelled peanuts for seed 48Ƀ, which is $2.40.) The labor involved was mostly Holy Day's. She worked alone for a week to build up the ridges of dirt in which the peanuts are planted, and then she watered the fields and put in the seed. When the crop was ready to be harvested, Holy Day arranged for help from her friends and relatives on a small-scale version of the "take a day, return a day" system. Charmer and Spin Out Gold helped Holy Day to uproot the peanuts, and New Dawn, Spin Out Gold, and Charmer, as well as three friends of Holy Day's from other families, helped with the process of separating the peanuts from the parent plants. This obligated Holy Day to return the amount of labor she received by helping the other young women when they needed it, but she didn't have to give them any money. When the peanuts were ready, Holy Day took them to the cheerful man who runs the Chiangmai Village peanut mill. He paid her for the peanuts by weight, deducting a small sum for the milling, and she received 195 Ƀ, or $9.75. Holy Day was reasonably pleased. After expenses, her profit on the peanut growing was 103 Ƀ, or $5.15. She gave 25 Ƀ to her mother, ($1.25, almost a quarter of her profits), and then she gave 5 Ƀ ($.25) to Grandmother Worth. The other 73 Ƀ she kept for herself. She spent some of it on clothes, and some at fairs.

Holy Day's peanut growing was entirely her own enterprise, rather than the family's, since the initial capital was her own, the land she used did not belong to the family, and the labor she exchanged was her own responsibility, not the whole family's. Sometimes the Plenitude children do use the family's land, or seed saved from the previous year's crop, but then the proportion of the profits which goes to Father Good and Mother Celestial as duty and respect money is much higher. Recently Older Sister Blessing grew garlic using the family's land. She used the family's seed garlic, too. She spent 300 Ƀ ($15.00) of her own on fertilizer, and she had Spin Out Gold, Holy Day, and Keen to help her, with the understanding that they would be paid a share of the profits, rather than having their labor returned. When the crop was ripe, Father Come, the headman of the southern half of the village, bought it for 2,000 ฿ ($100.00), unharvested, the arrangement being that he would bring in his own people to harvest. Older Sister Blessing subtracted the 300 ฿ which she had spent on fertilizer, and divided up the remaining 1,700 ฿ ($85.00). She distributed 200 ฿ ($10.00) each to herself, Spin Out Gold, Holy Day, and Keen and 900 ฿ ($45.00), more than 50 percent of the profits, to Father Good and Mother Celestial.

If the profits on an enterprise are very low, the person who earned the money may keep it all without giving any to Father Good and Mother Celestial. Holy Day, after an unfortunate experience with soybeans, was left with a net profit of 54.50 ฿ ($2.72½) for a season's work. She kept it herself, and used it for a trip to see an old friend whose family had emigrated from Chiangmai Village to a district called Faang, in the north, where the land is not as good, but the population is far less dense.

Both Older Sister Blessing and Spin Out Gold have pigs fattening in the thatch-roofed pigpen behind Older Sister Clear's house. They buy the pigs when they are mere piglets, brought into the village by itinerant salesmen. The salesmen transport the piglets from place to place in openwork baskets which are lashed to the backs of bicycles, a precarious ride for the piglet. The piglet sellers usually return when the pig is grown and make an offer to buy it back for slaughter. The pigs are fed on rice polishings, some of which are a byproduct of the rice the family eats, but the person who is raising the pig always has to buy more. Spin Out Gold says that pig raising never yields high profits, but it is a little like making regular deposits in a savings bank. A new piglet costs about 300 ฿ ($15.00), and after a year, when it has grown fatter on regular deposits of rice polishings, the selling price is around 1,000 ฿ ($50.00), only a little more than the cost of raising it.

The pig can always be sold sooner, if there is a need for ready cash. But occasionally the pig sickens and dies, and the whole enterprise is a failure.

In August, when the lamjajs (*Euphoria longana*) are ripe, there are jobs available harvesting the fruit. Lamjajs grow high on spreading trees, so they have to be picked from a ladder. They are about the size of a lychee, and are covered with a tough tan skin, which protects the moist grayish-white fruit inside. The lamjaj crop is sold by the tree, unharvested, and the lamjaj buyers hire work crews to gather what they have purchased. The crews are told where to meet each day, and they come on their bicycles or motorcycles at dawn. Lamjaj harvesting is considered an amusing job. Lots of young people work together (men climb the trees and throw down the fruit, while women clean, sort and pack) and there is the fun of going around to many different places all over the district in the course of the job. People who work well are hired back the next year at a better salary.

Moonlight has had jobs in the lamjaj harvest. The first season she worked, Moonlight cleaned the lamjajs, taking leaves off the harvested branches; the next year she started off as a cleaner, but was promoted to sorting the lamjajs for size; the third year she started as a sorter and was promoted to packing the lamjajs tightly into the huge cylindrical baskets, painted in red with the Chinese characters of the buyer's name, in which they are shipped. Moonlight doesn't remember how much she made the first year, but the second year her salary was 460 ฿ ($23.00) for a little more than a month's work, and the third year it rose to 780 ฿ ($39.00). The second year she worked, Moonlight got a job for Keen, too. He sewed up the baskets after they were packed. The third year New Dawn came along, and worked as a cleaner. The lamjaj picking jobs are only available in years with a lamjaj crop; in 1969, there were no lamjajs because the crop failed, and hence no jobs.

Some jobs are available within the village. When it is time to plant garlic, villagers hire groups of young girls to do the work for them at so much per area planted. These arrangements are usually made by women. For example, a friend of the Plenitudes may tell Holy Day that she wants about half an acre of land planted to garlic, and that she will pay 35 ฿ ($1.75) for the job. Then Holy Day will get a group of four or five people together, asking her sisters and Older Sister Clear's daughters first and her close friends second. When the job is done, the people who worked divide the money equally. Planting garlic is not hard, and it tends to be a specialty of teenaged girls. It isn't likely that Moonlight or Older Sister Blessing would plant garlic any more, although they both have in the past. Instead Holy Day, or Charmer, or Red would be asked first.

Moonlight's hairdressing project was paid for from the profits of many gardens, animals, and temporary jobs. She says that Father Good and Mother Celestial were unwilling to spend any of their money to have her trained, because of their bad experience with Older Sister Fine Qualities. (Older Sister Fine Qualities, who is dead now, dropped out of secondary school without finishing, so there was nothing to show for the money which had been spent on her education.) Moonlight spent 400 ฿ of her own for tuition. The hairdressing school was at the nearby market village of Road's Entrance, and Moonlight would go over in the morning on her bicycle. Another girl from Chiangmai Village went too and they had a very good time. The first lesson was rolling hair on rollers, and when Moonlight could do that well, she was permitted to go on to cutting and trimming by the use of a razor. Each pupil was allowed to practice on ten non-paying customers, before she advanced to paying customers. In three months the course was finished, and there was a graduation ceremony for the pupils. The formal picture taken at this ceremony is the one on the wall of the big main room of the Plenitudes' house.

Moonlight is quite proud of it. In the picture, her hair, and the hair of all the other pupils, is dressed most elegantly, and adorned with flowers.

After the graduation, Father Good and Mother Celestial were pleased with Moonlight. Father Good decided to make the big mirrored armoire (which is now part of the upstairs furniture) for her to use. The armoire is designed so that customers can sit in front of it and watch what Moonlight is doing, and there are shelves and drawers to store curlers, combs, and lotions. Moonlight had the armoire set up under the house, where it is cool and breezy and convenient for customers. She spent 1,000 ฿ ($50.00) on equipment and supplies. Since people in Chiangmai Village do not admire tawny tones or red highlights in hair, a large proportion of Moonlight's business consisted of dyeing hair a darker black. The hairdressing business was successful enough to create many fumes in the courtyard, fumes of shampoo and setting lotion and hairspray, and this was what brought it to an end. Grandfather Ten Thousand was in his last illness, and the smells made him feel worse, so he asked Moonlight to stop. Moonlight herself had begun to feel queasy from the fumes and perhaps a little bored with being a hairdresser day after day. She was willing to do as he told her. Now she cuts and dyes hair for her family and an occasional friend, but not as a business, and not very often. Moonlight is saving for a new project; she wants to go to dressmaking school, and have a sewing machine, like Tender Gold, who lives next door. Then she could make dresses, bras, blouses, and slacks, and spend more or less time at it depending on the pressures of the rice-growing season. She is thinking of keeping her sewing machine in Tender Gold's house, when she gets it, so that they could sew together companionably.

Keen has been the beneficiary of a big project to train village youth. He was chosen out of the Village Youth Group to go to the Thai-German Dairy, which is an international cooperative project in Chiengmai. He learned how to take care of the dairy cows they keep there, but the villagers do not keep cows or enjoy drinking milk, and his training is not useful in Chiangmai Village. He also learned how to raise chickens under electric light. Mother Celestial liked that part of his training, because she would go to see him, and he would give her lots of free eggs. However, it would not be reasonable to raise chickens under electric light in the village, because the cost of electricity is prohibitively expensive. Most families do not want to pay for more than what is used by one electric bulb at a time. Keen has been able to find other jobs in Chiengmai. Once he went to work on a construction project at the university, painting walls. He earned 20 ฿ ($1.00) a day, an average wage. The understanding was that he would only be paid every time he completed fifteen days' work—not necessarily fifteen consecutive days, but a total of fifteen, so that he could take one day off to sow rice at home, and return to work in town the next. Keen hears about jobs like this through his friends, and they go to work as a group.

Spin Out Gold has a part-time job in the village. She helps a woman called Older Sister Precious with cooking, washing and sweeping, drawing water, and keeping house. Older Sister Precious approves of Spin Out Gold's boyfriend and lets him visit Spin Out Gold at work. This is a face-saving arrangement for everyone concerned. It spares Father Good and Mother Celestial from having to countenance publicly a relationship which they have tried to end, and it spares Spin Out Gold and her boyfriend the inhibitions and embarrassments of meeting with Father Good and Mother Celestial nearby. Spin Out Gold gets money and presents of cloth from Older Sister Precious, but the value of the job is largely in freeing her from the constraints of home.

Trading at the markets is yet another economic opportunity for the Plenitudes. It is a job for women, so much so that a man in the marketplace, unless he is a Chinese trader rather than a Northern Thai peasant, is an uncommon sight. People from Chiangmai Village can go to the small village markets, the larger market of the market town, or the great markets of Chiengmai, which are positively cosmopolitan in the selection of goods offered and the variety of customers who come. The markets all meet every day, rather than in cycles every few days. The best selection is available before dawn, and the village and market-town markets are usually sold out by mid-morning, although the markets of Chiengmai run all day.

The nearest market to Chiangmai Village is the village market at Orchard Grove, which is about fifteen minutes away by bicycle, across a small river. The market place consists of a large square, roofed over, and furnished with long rows of wooden tables. The market is owned by a Chinese trader of Orchard Grove. All of the women set out their wares on the wooden tables, and in the course of the market a man who works for the Chinese trader comes by and collects a small fee for the use of the space. At Orchard Grove, women come to sell the tiny shrimps they have caught in the canals, or vegetables they have grown, or hot sweet cakes which they make on the spot. They also sell packages of tobacco, which the purchasers make into cheroots, and mîaŋ. Mîaŋ is the name for fermented tea leaves, and people love to chew it with rock salt; it is an indispensable part of any Northern Thai gathering and is always offered to guests. The women of Chiangmai Village shop at Orchard Grove, but they do not usually sell there, because the prices are a fraction lower than at any of the other nearby markets. Some women buy packages of tobacco at Orchard Grove, perhaps four packages at half a baht (2½¢) each, bring them back to Chiangmai Village, repackage them so there are five packages, and sell them again at another market at half a baht per package. The best village market for selling is the market at Road's Entrance. Road's Entrance is the place where Mother Celestial used to sell when she was a market woman. It is across the fields in

19. The village market at Orchard Grove.

the opposite direction from Orchard Grove. Mother Celestial
used to rise before dawn and carry her wares to market
through the dark, sometimes taking one of the children to help
her. She did not usually buy at Orchard Grove to repackage
and sell at Road's Entrance, since the profit is so small;
besides she always had plenty of coconuts and vegetables from
her own courtyard and garden to sell. Mother Celestial was a

market woman for years, and only stopped when her bad knee made the long walk to market too painful.

The market town nearest to Chiangmai Village is called Nodding Rubber Trees. The market there is bigger than the village markets at Orchard Grove or Road's Entrance, and full of variety. It is owned by a Chinese trader too. At Nodding Rubber Trees there are butchers selling pork. (The villagers eat meat; although Buddhism is theoretically opposed to taking life, they feel that they are not morally accountable if someone else does the slaughtering. There is a proverb which says, "If it weren't for bad people, good people couldn't eat chopped meat.") The prices at Nodding Rubber Trees are slightly higher again. Moonlight has tried selling there. She sold roasted coconuts, a delightful snack: the thin sweet juice to drink and then the custardy flesh to eat, all with a warm, toasty flavor from being roasted over coals.

Older Sister Clear and Older Sister Blessing have decided that it is worth their while to go all the way to the great market place called the Lamjaj Market in Chiengmai, rather than to one of the smaller markets nearby. At the Lamjaj Market the prices are another notch higher, and there are large crowds of shoppers. Older Sister Blessing goes to the market only when she is not needed in the rice fields, but Older Sister Clear goes every day. Older Sister Clear's day as market woman begins the afternoon before, when she assembles the different things she will take to market. She goes around to the houses of friends who have produce to sell, and buys up coconuts, banana leaves, eggs, and edible vines with little tendrils. She brings them back to the courtyard and adds her own produce to the pile, setting everything out on a low wooden platform under her little house. In the evenings she sits on the platform, and prepares the produce for sale by the light of a single electric bulb which is attached to the side of the house. Older Sister Clear husks her coconuts, and decides whether to roast them or leave them green; the roasted ones are more trouble

20. Older Sister Clear preparing the banana leaves for market.

for her, but bring a higher price. She wraps the edible vines neatly in packages made of envelopes of banana leaf held together with a splinter of wood, so that the tendrils curl attractively over the top of each package. She spreads out the banana leaves, wipes them with a cloth, folds them in thirds, and packs them in stacks in her basket. People will buy them to use as wrapping paper or cooking parchment. Many friends and relatives drop by to talk to her as she works, since evening is the usual time for recreation in Chiangmai Village. By the time Older Sister Clear is finished, everyone has gone home and the courtyard is dark. She is the last to go to bed.

In the morning, she has to rise the earliest, since the man who owns the village taxi (a small pickup truck with a roof and benches installed in the back) leaves at 4:30 A.M. He has a standing agreement to take her and the other market women of Chiangmai Village to the Lamjaj Market each morning. When they arrive at the market, it is just beginning to get light. Older Sister Clear does not sit at a table in the covered part of the market. Instead, she has made an arrangement with a woman who runs a little restaurant across the street.

She sits on the pavement in front of the restaurant, and avoids the higher fee for a space in the market place itself. Twenty market women or more share this pavement with her and form an extension of the market place. They are not under cover if it rains, but plenty of shoppers go by and see the things they have to sell. Older Sister Clear arranges her wares on two circular trays which fit over the top of her baskets. Then she sits behind the baskets against the wall of the shop. On most days she sells out by 9:30 or 10:00 A.M., and she gathers up her baskets and trays, meets the taxi, and goes home with the other Chiangmai Village market women.

All of these ways of making a living—the major enterprise of rice growing and all of the smaller enterprises—demand a great deal of hard work, day after day, in order to gain the bare possibility of succeeding. There is no way to be sure of success itself. Every member of the Plenitude family feels an undercurrent of anxiety that there will not be enough rice or enough money. All of them have seen many enterprises fail. Their daily tensions are different from but just as unpleasant as the tensions of other ways of life, and the life they lead as rice-farming peasants is far from bucolic.

A Working Day

I have discussed the family as an economic unit, sharing the common enterprise of rice growing, and as a group of individuals with economic enterprises of their own. I have not yet shown how economic life is managed on the day-to-day level: how time is spent, and to what end, when people work, and when they rest and eat, nor have I described the shape and qualities of a working day. For these purposes I have chosen a day at the beginning of the rice growing season, when there is still time for Older Sister Blessing to go to the market, but when demands for labor in the rice fields are beginning to be increasingly urgent.

In the early morning, before dawn, Older Sister Blessing got up while everyone else in the big house was still sleeping. She put on her white blouse, and wrapped a long pale green skirt around her waist, fastening it with a silver link belt. She took her two baskets filled with fruit for the market and the carrying stick to hang them from, and crept quietly out of the house to meet Older Sister Clear in the courtyard. Together the two of them waited in the dark for the village taxi, and when it came they climbed into the back and drove off to the market; the red tail lights of the taxi winked and bounced down the lane, and they were gone. For a time the courtyard was dark and quiet again, but as dawn began to break, Mother Celestial got out of bed. She put on a white blouse and a skirt with a pattern of wavy brown points and magenta flowers. She climbed down the back stairs, and began to sweep the court-yard with a heavy broom made of twigs bound around a stick. The long rhythmic scratch, scratch, of that broom is a characteristic early morning noise every day of the year.

Up in the house, Grandmother Worth, Holy Day, and Spin Out Gold, Moonlight, Keen, and Father Good, stirred and began to get up. Holy Day knew that she had the job of steaming the rice, so she went into the kitchen, built up the cooking fire, took the glutinous rice from the green crock where it had soaked overnight, and put it to steam. Spin Out Gold took a dustcloth and the curved, fluffy broom which is used indoors. She swept, wiped, and dusted through the whole house, a job which has to be done every day, because the dust comes in through the open windows, and the little lizards which run over the walls and ceilings leave messy droppings on the cabinets and the polished floors. Father Good came out of his bedroom. He was wearing one of the dark blue shirts with four pockets which Northern Thai villagers wear for everyday, and a long, old-fashioned man's sarong of a pleasant blue plaid pattern. (Father Good's sarong is a flat piece of cloth, not sewn into a tube like a woman's skirt; if he likes, he can use it as a loin cloth.) Father Good spoke to Keen who was still in bed under his mosquito net in the alcove of the main room. He pointed out that it was well past time to get up. Keen grunted an answer. He and his father have had words on this subject almost every morning for some time past.

Then Father Good went outside, through the courtyard, and over the irrigation canal into the fields, to the little field which was going to be used as a seed bed. He planned to flood it that day. Keen got out of his comfortable bed and dressed himself, in old black pants of the modern sort and a modern shirt, not a blue one like his father's. He followed his father to the seed bed, and began to set up the motor pump which the family had borrowed for the flooding.

Back at the house, Moonlight had dressed in a cream-colored blouse and one of her workday skirts. The skirt was patterned most splendidly with a design of a large bird, red, with flowing tail, perched gracefully beside a brown nest filled with eggs, against a smaller background pattern in red and white. Since Older Sister Blessing was gone, Moonlight took over the job of making breakfast. She decided that they would eat a cold dressed cucumber salad, and began to prepare the ingredients: boiled duck eggs, chopped peanuts, pickled onions, scallions, celery, tomatoes, little tropical limes, round aromatic green leaves, pieces of pork and pork fat, cucumbers and hot red pepper sauce. As Moonlight worked, Holy Day took the steamed rice off the fire, spread it in a great flat wooden rice tray to cool, and then packed it into covered baskets to keep during the day.

New Dawn was up, and wearing one of the skirts she prefers, horizontal stripes in shades of lavender, with a wide black border at the hem. (This is a traditional Northern Thai garment, like Father Good's blue shirt.) New Dawn carried a pile of dirty laundry down to the bathing enclosure. She drew water from the well and filled her plastic washtub, then poured in some Fab and began to scrub. Holy Day, who had finished with the rice, came out of the house and fed her ducks. When they had eaten she turned them out in a flock for their day of paddling and foraging in the rice fields.

By 7:30 Moonlight had finished making the breakfast, and the members of the family came up to the kitchen, one by one, to eat. They sat on the floor around the big common dishes of rice and cold salad and the little dishes of sauce. Using their fingers, they scooped up little wads of sticky rice and dipped them into the salad and sauce before eating them. Each person got up and left to go about the business of the day as soon as he or she was full. In the village it is not considered more polite to wait for the others before starting or finishing a meal; people eat at their own speed and leave whenever they wish.

It was about 8:20 A.M. when Keen went back to the field, taking his hoe, to straighten the raised earthen dykes which keep the water from flowing out of the field once it has been pumped in. Father Good rested for a little after his breakfast. At 9:30 he went out to work with Keen. When Holy Day had finished eating, she went downstairs, drew water from the well and began to fill all of the family's water jars—the big jars on the open platform by the kitchen, the little jars of drinking water, one in the courtyard and one at the landing of the front stairs, and the jars which stand at the foot of the stairs, both front and back, from which people can dip water to wash their feet before they enter the house. Moonlight put away the breakfast things and took out the iron. She filled it with hot coals from the fire, and began to iron the clothes which had been washed and dried the day before. She sat on the floor of the main room, with a thick smooth folded cloth laid out in front of her as a surface to iron on.

Spin Out Gold filled a pair of baskets with unmilled rice from the granary in the middle of the courtyard. She balanced the baskets from the carrying stick over her shoulder, and set off for the rice mill near the temple. There they have a milling machine which separates the husk from the grain.

Holy Day finished filling the water jars. Then she brought out her own dirty clothes and began to wash them. Each daughter washes her own clothes and then helps wash the clothes of Father Good, Keen, Mother Celestial, and Grandmother Worth, so that they do not have to do their own laundry. The daughters have an agreement that clean skirts can be borrowed on condition that the borrower washes and irons the skirt she has used and returns it to the owner's pile. All skirts are the same size. Holy Day, who is tiny and delicate, can wear the same skirt as Older Sister Blessing, who is tall and heavy, by wrapping it to fit with a deeper fold in the front. When Holy Day had finished her washing, she hung the clothes to dry on the lines which zigzag across the courtyard. Since New Dawn's washing was already on the lines, everyone who crossed the courtyard had to dodge and duck or go around.

Spin Out Gold came back from the rice mill. She took some of the milled husks and mixed them with water to feed to the pigs. Frantic squeals rose from the pigpen, subsiding into snuffles and grunts as the troughs were filled.

At 11:00 or so Older Sister Blessing and Older Sister Clear came back from the market. Older Sister Blessing had sold all of her fruit, and now her baskets contained only some little packages of spice and pork which she had bought. Older Sister Clear had sold everything too. Mother Celestial greeted her and Older Sister Blessing and began examining all of Older Sister Blessing's packages. Older Sister Clear crossed the courtyard and wearily climbed the rickety wooden ladder into her own house. Then Mother Celestial and Older Sister Blessing went up the back stairs into their house to begin working on the lunch. The heat of the day had begun to bear down on the fields and the courtyard, and everyone was starting to be hungry and tired. Older Sister Blessing and Mother Celestial prepared the ingredients for spicy stir-fried cabbage. They took pork and pepper, little green chili peppers, shrimp paste and fish paste, garlic, monosodium glutamate, cabbage, and oil made by rendering pork fat. They cut up the pork and the cabbage, made a spicy sauce from the other ingredients, and stir-fried everything together in the oil. This they served with steamed rice from the covered baskets, and as the family members finished their jobs, they washed and came to the kitchen to eat.

After lunch everyone sat under the house, where it seems a little cooler, some on the platform and some on the bench of split bamboo, listening to the radio and talking. Father Good decided that some of the daughters should come out to the seed bed and start the job of puddling it. Keen had more work to do on the dykes. Around 2:00 P.M. Keen went back to the field, and Holy Day went with him to start the puddling. Older Sister Blessing felt too tired from her early start and her morning at the market to work in the field. She decided to have a rest first. Father Good was tired from his morning, and he stayed in the courtyard and rested, too. Spin Out Gold went to help Older Sister Precious, the woman she works for. After a while, Older Sister Blessing felt better. She thought she would go and help Holy Day in the seed bed, and New Dawn went with her. Holy Day came back to the courtyard at 5:00, and Keen at 5:30, but Older Sister Blessing and New Dawn stayed in the field until after 6:00, when the sun was low in the sky behind the mountains.

In the kitchen, Moonlight and Mother Celestial had been working on the supper, which was to consist of raw chopped water buffalo meat and flavored broth. They made the broth by simmering entrails in water. Then they made a mixture of roasted dried chili peppers, some rough red seed pods shaped like miniature sausages which grow on a tree and are hot to the taste, and a small quantity of blended spice purchased from the market (one of the spices in the blend is star anise), and they pounded all these to powder with a mortar and pestle. They added little cubes of a white root which is shaped like ginger root, and lemon grass, shrimp paste, garlic and salt. They cooked all of these things together. They put the piece of meat on the round chopping block and chopped it with the cleaver, over and over again, first chopping one way and then another, until it was almost a paste. Then they mixed the raw meat with the cooked seasonings, and put it out in serving dishes along with the broth and the rest of the steamed rice from the covered rice baskets. Everyone likes chopped meat. It is a Northern Thai specialty and a favorite dish.

While they were cooking, the members of the family came back to the courtyard, one by one. Each person bathed before supper, drawing water from the well, carrying it to the bathing enclosure, and scooping it up with a small bowl to pour over him or herself. There was a lot of splashing, and a miasma of scented soap, which everyone loves, spread over the courtyard, to mingle with the spicy cloud drifting down from the kitchen. After bathing each person changed into clean clothes, the clothes that would be worn the next day, too, and went up-stairs for supper. Everyone relaxed with a cool bath and a good supper, and enjoyed the slight diminution of heat which had come with the evening. After the meal, they sat around and talked. Evening is the time of recreation and visiting. Some nights there is a medicine show at the temple, and some nights groups of young men come calling. Often Keen leaves with a group of male friends to go and call on girls in other villages. On this night Father Good went to bed early. Mother Celestial, Older Sister Blessing, and Moonlight crossed the courtyard to chat with Older Sister Clear as she prepared for the next day's market, and Older Sister Valuable crossed the lane to chat with them. New Dawn and Holy Day stayed up-stairs. Some young men came to call for Keen, and they went up to talk to Holy Day and New Dawn for a little while before they left. Then the group under Older Sister Clear's house broke up, leaving her there alone, and the others headed for their beds and a night's rest. Gradually the courtyard became quiet and dark, as everyone settled to sleep. There was a muffled noise around midnight, as Keen came back from his evening out, and then everything was still. The moon shone with a white glare through the stiff spiked pinwheels of the palm trees, a dog barked and was silent, and a long while later, a water buffalo in a nearby courtyard stirred, blew out— whoosh—through his nostrils, shifted position, and was quiet again.

4

The Family and the Temple

*Structure and Individuality in a
Larger Institutional Context*

The single most important social institution in the village is
the temple. It symbolizes the unity of the village, in spite of
the factionalization which splits the northern half of Chiangmai Village from the southern half, and it symbolizes the village's cultural ties to the Buddhism of the Great Tradition.
But I do not wish to consider the temple from these points of
view, which have been discussed by Kingshill (1965), Moerman (1966), and Tambiah (1970), but from another point of
view: as a major institutional context in which the members
of the family act. In the preceding chapter I have shown the
interplay between the social structure of family life and the
individuality of the members of the family in a variety of
economic contexts: each person moving, in his or her own idio-
syncratic way, through a culturally established pattern of
obligations and expectations which has the force to shape
lives. Now I would like to show the interplay between family
structure, individuality, and an institution larger than the

83

family. Beyond the smaller social world of the courtyard the temple is perhaps the most important social context for family members. Yet each family member experiences the temple differently, and acts differently in the context of temple life, which offers many choices.

The Chiangmai Village Temple is the geographical as well as the social center of the village. It is a graceful, pillared building with decorated eaves and mosaics of colored mirror glass, and it stands in a courtyard of its own. The temple courtyard is surrounded, not by hedges or fences, but by buildings which serve the village as a whole. There is a long yellow stucco school building, a new, pink two-story building which houses the monk and novices, and two tile-roofed pavilions without walls which serve as meeting halls. Then there is the communal kitchen, where villagers prepare quantities of food for temple festivals, and a low shed which holds a set of gongs in graduated sizes, and drums of various types. Both gongs and drums are used to summon the villagers to meetings, and to beat out the music to which the village dancers perform. The largest drum is called ʔIi Koŋ Kham, Golden Lady, and it is beaten by the villagers at the annual drumming contest between Chiangmai Village and other villages held at the District Office in Saraphii town.

The temple is generous in the wide variety of activities it provides, and each person participates in his or her own way. The old people of the village are most assiduous participants in temple activities, and Grandmother Worth is the most faithful member of the Plenitude family. When there is a time of religious importance, like the beginning of the Buddhist lenten season (the period when the monks are restricted to the temple), Grandmother Worth dresses formally in a white blouse, with a white scarf wrapped diagonally over it, and a black or grey silk skirt, and goes with the other old people to listen to sermons and sleep overnight at the temple, an act of piety which earns religious merit. She brings a mat to sleep on, and the children bring food from home for her at mealtimes. The old people enjoy being together and socializing. As Moon-light says, the old people don't need a social club, they have the temple. Often the priest reads tales of morality to them and they discuss the meaning of the tales and other religious subjects. Sometimes the tales emphasize the importance of

21. The Temple.

22. An interior view of the Temple.

23. The Golden Lady drum.

24. Preparing food for a temple festival.

avoiding conflict; at other times they stress the theme of the importance of respect for old people, a subject which the audience has at heart. Once the priest told this tale:

> Once upon a time, a man went out fishing. He caught a wonderful huge fish, and when he had brought it home, he curried it and shared it with all his fellow villagers. Everyone was glad to take it, except for one old woman who said, "Don't eat any of that fish, I warn you." She threw hers out. The other villagers heard her, but they looked at one another and said, "Fish curry is fish curry, and this looks fine to me." They ate it with pleasure. The next morning the earth opened up and swallowed every house in that village except the house of the old lady who had given the warning. That enormous fish had been the guardian of the village and it was offended at having been caught and eaten. This tale tells us to pay attention to old people and listen to them with respect, because they may know something we don't know.

When Grandmother Worth came home, she repeated this tale to the family.

Participating in religious ceremonies and festivals is a great delight to Grandmother Worth, and has been for a long time. One of her favorite subjects of conversation is the time, many years ago, when she went on a temple-sponsored pilgrimage to Dɔɔj Suthêb, one of the blue mountains visible from Chiangmai Village, and visited the beautiful temple which looks like a tiny gold toy on its distant slope. "We went around to Dɔɔj Suthêb," she likes to say, making vague circles in the air with her hand. "We took milled rice with us, and we didn't come home until it was all gone." Grandmother Worth likes to go to ceremonies in nearby villages, too. Dressed in her formal clothes and perched precariously on the back of a bicycle pedalled by Older Brother Eye, her granddaughter Older Sister Clear's husband, she goes off to events like the ordination of her mother's sister's grandchild in the neighboring village of Crystal Rise, with Moonlight calling out, "Sit tight, Granny!" as they wobble away. Later, the Plenitudes begin to receive reports about her: that she is having a good time; or that there were so many people that she didn't get a wink of sleep; that she liked the festival food; and that she spent all afternoon listening to the local comic opera, which is done in Commedia del'Arte style, and is considered very funny.

All fairs are connected with the temple, and Grandmother Worth loves fairs, too. Once the Ferris Wheel came to Chiangmai Village as part of a fair. It was set up in front of the temple, decorated with neon lights. Villagers set up stalls to sell sweets and dried cuttlefish, and actors performed on the rickety little leaf-roofed stage just outside of the temple courtyard. Grandmother Worth found herself a comfortable place to sit at the foot of a palm tree, and spent all evening watching the people come and go, and peering at the Ferris Wheel. For Grandmother Worth the temple is a source of genuine pleasure which is valued even more because it is defined as religious.

Father Good's involvement with the temple is quite a different thing from Grandmother Worth's. He is on the Temple's School Committee. Traditionally, schools in Thailand were run by monks; and they are still closely associated with temples as is the case in Chiangmai Village. This committee is an important setting for village politics, since it is made up of the richest and most powerful men in the village, representatives of every faction. Father Good spends a great deal of time at the committee meetings. For him the temple is essentially a political forum, in which the prominent men of Chiangmai Village jockey for position, form alliances, intrigue, come to the brink of open quarreling, and then retrieve the situation. They do not care to discuss the details of local politics with outsiders, but much of the political action revolves around questions of temple policy and appropriation of funds.

Father Good's loyalties are partly determined by the division of the village into a northern faction and a southern faction. These two halves of the village have different headmen and different administrative designations. When there is difficulty between the two halves of the village, Father Good's loyalties are with the south, where his house and the houses of his closest friends and allies are located. Father Good's loyalties are also partly to individuals who are his friends and allies. These people are linked with him by three main kinds of structural ties: membership in the same neighborhood group, membership in the same agricultural labor exchange group, and membership in the group which worships the same matrilineally inherited ancestral spirits (these will be discussed in detail later), or membership in all these kinds of groups at once. Father Good's closest friend and ally is Father Seeker, the assistant headman of the southern half of the village, who is also on the School Committee. Father Seeker lives adjacent to the Plenitudes on the north side of the courtyard, so he is a near neighbor, and he shares both the other kinds of social ties—exchange of labor and common spirit group membership—with them. He is the one who rents land to Older Sister Clear's husband Older Brother Eye. Another important ally of Father Good's, not so close but more powerful, is Father Come, the headman of the southern half of the village. (Father Seeker is his assistant.) He lives near Father Good, four or five courtyards away, and exchanges agricultural labor with him, but since his family's protective spirits are different, he is allied with a different matrilineal group. Father Good and Father Come exchange a variety of favors. For example, Father Come helped Moonlight and New Dawn to get jobs he heard of, and then several months later, Father Good and Mother Celestial sold their garlic crop to him rather than to one of the other garlic buyers.

These three political allies, namely Father Good, Father Seeker, and the headman, Father Come, are on one side of a tangled controversy over some missing funds which can serve as an example of the sort of tensions which are played out in the committee, and as an example of the way Father Good acts politically with his allies. The funds had been collected by

Father Seeker, in his capacity as assistant headman of the southern half of the village, and allegedly handed over by him to the assistant headman of the northern half of the village. The assistant headman of the northern half of the village was supposed to give the money to a government agency, so that the agency would provide electric light poles for the villagers under a matching funds program. The money never reached the agency. Father Seeker and Father Come claimed that the assistant headman of the northern half of the village had taken the money for himself. The assistant headman claimed that he took the money to the agency but it was closed for lunch. His patron, the wealthy retired village head of the northern half of the village, claimed that *he* was holding the funds, in a sort of escrow for future payment. The priest, allied with the northern half of the village by birth and family ties, denounced Father Come over the temple public address system as an irreligious maker of irresponsible accusations. Father Come, Father Seeker, and Father Good were very angry, but did not express that anger openly. The truth is lost in the confusion of charge and countercharge. This working out of factionalism and alliance in a politico-religious forum is of endless interest to Father Good. This is the way he involves himself in the temple as an institution. It is in accordance with his position at the head of a relatively wealthy and powerful family.

Mother Celestial's main interests in the temple are connected with food: donating food for the monk and the eight or ten novices, and helping to prepare food for temple feasts. Mother Celestial is the sort of person who is interested in food, interested both in eating it and talking about it. She likes to swap recipes, and her account of an occasion usually includes a description of what was eaten and whether it was good or not. She is willing to spend extra money to have special tidbits brought back from the big market in Chiengmai—ocean fish, or special spices—and this is a rare attitude in Chiangmai Village, where one of the best ways of saving money is by eating only foods which have been grown or caught on the spot.

Mother Celestial is in charge of one of the seven groups of villagers which send food and rice to the temple on succeeding days. Chiangmai Village has been geographically divided into seven sections to form these groups, and one person is in charge of each section. The person in charge, who is a woman resident of the section, has the responsibility of beating a gong the afternoon before the food is to be donated, so that all of her neighbors will be reminded. The cycle is irregular, because one day each week is a Buddhist holy day, when everyone in the village contributes, and there are seven sections; the regular cycle picks up where it left off when the holy day is over. Mother Celestial beats the gong in the early afternoon, about 1:30 or 2:00 P.M., standing on her front steps. The family dogs stand at her feet and howl at the gong. The next morning early, Holy Day or Spin Out Gold carries the Plenitudes' contribution to the temple, and others from the same section who are making donations meet them in the temple kitchen: they all empty their enamel lunch boxes, which are made like a series of stacking bowls, into the temple's big dishes. This custom of bringing the food to the temple, rather than having the monk and novices go out to beg each morning, is a variant in Buddhist practice. Some, but not all, of the nearby villages bring food to the temples as the people of Chiangmai Village do; but in other villages, the monks may be seen each morning, with begging bowls, helping villagers to obtain religious merit by accepting alms. Chiangmai Village people say that the present monk felt that bringing food to the temple would be more convenient for himself and for the villagers, and so this method was adopted. (Another Chiangmai Village custom is to allow the novices an evening meal at home with their families; usually neither monk nor novice is supposed to take food after the noon meal.)

Being in charge of the food-sending section is a regular responsibility of Mother Celestial's. She also helps to prepare festival food for the temple. On occasions such as donation festivals, when groups of people representing other temples come and contribute to the Chiangmai Village temple, the villagers are expected to prepare food for the visitors. Usually the menu consists of steamed rice, a curry (perhaps of water buffalo meat), and another dish, which might be a kind of local coleslaw with ground peanuts as garnish. The temple owns enough cooking utensils and crockery to prepare for and serve the food to the guests. The people who are going to cook gather in the temple courtyard before the festival. Some watch the hollowed tree trunk vessels in which great quantities of glutinous rice are steamed over low, wide-mouthed black pots of boiling water. Others sit over an indoor hearth in the low kitchen building next to the drum shed, chopping the meat and pounding the spices for the curry, which is made in great woks three feet across. Young girls are given the job of cleaning and chopping vegetables. Mother Celestial gives directions, discusses proportions, and presses her advice on the other cooks. When the food is done she usually manages to take some home to her family. Other villagers have criticized her for this, but it is quite likely that all the cooks keep some of the food for themselves. Mother Celestial's participation in the temple activities is appropriate to her age, sex, and interests, and very different from her husband's participation or her mother's.

Older Sister Blessing's greatest contribution to temple activities is the making of special decorations. She is a virtuoso of paper flower making, and a poetess of crepe paper tassels. When the priest asks for new decorations for a festival, Older Sister Blessing brings out her sheets of soft, pastel-colored crepe paper, her big scissors, her wire and her thread. She cuts hundreds of oval paper rose petals and leaves, or little fringed strips that will be tassels. She shapes the crepe paper so that it curves like a petal, or ripples its edges to make a frill. Then, using thread and wire, she makes roses and orchids, or patriotic tassels in red, white, and blue with little gold flowers hanging from the ends. In one ceremony, each household is asked to donate a money tree to the temple. Each tree is decorated with paper flowers and crisp clean money (usually bills of small denomination so as to make a better show) and mounted on a wooden platform. Then the different sections of the village bring their trees, one from each courtyard, in a procession to the temple as the sun sets. Older Sister Blessing, with New Dawn's help, created a wonderful tree for the Plenitudes, with orchids in two shades of lavender. It took all of her free time for days. Bits of colored paper fluttered around the courtyard, clinging to people and animals, as Older Sister Blessing sat on the bamboo platform under the house, snipping and tying.

Older Sister Blessing also likes to make special sweets to be donated to the temple. The sweets are different kinds of sugared and flavored rice mixtures made into little banana leaf packages of various shapes and steamed. Sometimes the sweets are flavored with banana or grated coconut, sometimes tapioca is added. The packages are intricately folded, and Older Sister Blessing has to spend a lot of time cutting banana leaves into shape before the cooking begins. Helping to make these sweets is a popular diversion, and every girl or woman in the neighborhood with time to spare gathers around Older Sister Blessing on the Plenitudes' airy kitchen porch to help with the cutting of leaves, mixing of ingredients, and preparation of the little packages for steaming. Everyone tastes the sweets when they are ready, and early the next morning they are given to the temple.

Moonlight loves the temple for its formality. When she offers up flowers and popped rice, or makes the gesture of respect and reverence during the chanting, a flower in her fingertips, she creates a small artistic performance, both beautiful and correct. Her rice and flowers are offered in three gestures on each of the three offering plates. The flower held between her fingertips for the chanting is changed after it has been lowered at the end of the chant, because things which have been lowered are not as fine as things which have not been lowered. Her used flowers form a heap in front of her on the floor, while her fresh flowers diminish on the enamel plate at her side. When she was younger, Moonlight was a member of the group of dancers supported by the temple. Her pleasure in dancing was like her pleasure in ritual—the pleasure of a series of formal movements. If the dancer learns the pattern of movement, she knows she is beautiful. Nowadays, Moonlight helps to train the dancers. She is remarkably good at the performance of form and pattern: her dancing is a controlled system of beauty. And the connection in her mind between formality, correctness, and beauty, which appears in ritual and in dancing, applies also to her ideas of morality. She can accept a predetermined pattern which defines good and evil, and she believes that to follow the pattern is to behave beautifully and morally. She rejects the notion that there might be many different definitions of good and evil, or a wide variety of ideas about morality. She is happy to be able to behave beautifully by following a pattern, and she loves the pattern for its own sake.

New Dawn's main interest in the temple is also as a dancer, but she sees dancing quite differently: confident of her own grace and beauty, New Dawn adorns the dance rather than using it to adorn herself, like Moonlight, who is not so sure of her own loveliness. New Dawn enjoys the special costumes and the curved metal pieces worn on the fingers in the finger-nail dance, which the temple buys for the dancers. She enjoys participating, but she doesn't love the formality of the dance for its own sake. Dancing is a personal pleasure to her. She doesn't connect it with morality or patterns of beauty, the way Moonlight does. New Dawn has little in her character which predisposes her to be dedicated to forces or ideals outside of herself, nor is she willing to explain the meaning things have for her. Instead, she has a detachment and lightness of touch which the villagers value highly, because a person thus endowed escapes the suffering caused by emotional involvement and comes closer to the Buddhist ideal. Moonlight's heart is not detached, but she commits it to a system of values; the detached heart which is part of New Dawn's character makes her an integral part of the system, which values detachment more than commitment.

As for Keen, he has lived the life of a novice in the temple for two years, starting when he was fourteen. He entered the temple at the desire of Grandfather Ten Thousand, who was eager, for several important reasons, that Keen should be ordained. The life in the temple is easy, since there is no heavy work in the fields and gardens, and Grandfather Ten Thousand wanted Keen to have a pleasant time for a while longer, instead of taking on adult responsibilities. Also, as a novice, Keen's education would be continued without the expense of sending him to school outside the village. By the age of fourteen, Keen, like most village children, had already completed the four years of free compulsory schooling which are provided by the Chiangmai Village school. Also, the ordination of a novice brings religious merit to the sponsors of his ordination ceremony, and Grandfather Ten Thousand, who was already an old man, was pleased to make merit (for discussions of the significance of merit making see Kingshill [1965] and Phillips [1965] among others). The ceremony brings prestige to the novice's family, too. There is feasting and entertainment by musicians and singers, and people come from miles around to take part. Mother Celestial still displays a picture of Keen at his ordination. He stands, plump and placid (he was a fat little boy), dressed in the epicene finery of the "crystal child," as the candidate for ordination is called. The costume includes silk pants and sunglasses, and the crystal child is heavily made up with pale face powder, lipstick, and eyebrow pencil. Dressed and adorned, he parades through the village on a horse hired for the occasion, and at the conclusion of the

25. A "crystal child," with his sponsors and the donations they have made.

ceremonies he changes into the robes of a monk, glowing orange in color but of a draped simplicity of form. During the two years that Keen was a novice, he studied religious chants and charms, and helped the abbot to make the fireworks which the Chiangmai Village Temple produces both for sale and for use in ceremonies like funerals where evil spirits are to be frightened. There is some mystery about Keen's final departure from the life of a novice. Villagers imply that he committed some sort of irregularity, but no one will say what, and the Plenitudes avoid the subject altogether. Nowadays, Keen frequents the temple only for the meetings of youth

97

26. Keen as "crystal child" (extreme left).

groups to which he belongs. He is beginning to use the temple as a political arena the way his father does.

The members of the Plenitude family are neither theologians nor religious scholars. They wish to be moral people, but they do not care particularly about the intricacies and abstractions of Buddhism. They care deeply about their temple, but each one of them experiences the temple in an utterly different way. They act according to the expectations and requirements for strong fathers, old ladies, or beautiful young women, but they vary their actions according to their individuality and idiosyncracies, acting in a cultural context which is, in every case, extremely important to them. Yet in every case the interplay between culture and individuality produces a unique result.

5

The Order of
Social Relationships
in the Family

Social relationships in the Northern Thai family are ordered on three important principles: first, formal authority belongs to men rather than women; second, juniors must defer to seniors, and seniors take responsibility for the welfare of juniors; and third, family relationships are lineal, but with a kind of lineality which has not, to my knowledge, been previously reported in the anthropological literature. This is a lineality traced through women, where men are merely affinal members of a matriline of which women consanguineally related to one another are the core. (I have referred to this form of lineality earlier as a sort of mirror image of patriliny.) I wish to show how these three principles form the structural basis for the Plenitudes' family life, and at the same time to show how an individual's position in the structure directly affects his or her life experience.

Father Good is the head of the Plenitude family, since he is a man, and men, as the Thai proverb has it, are superior to women, just as the front legs of an elephant are superior to the hind legs. However, since his matriline membership is derived from his wife's family, and it is to them that he is responsible in using his authority, the authority he has is inherited affinally, from his father-in-law. Two of the important principles, the principle that formal authority belongs to men, and the principle that matriline membership comes from women, are interwoven here. The crucial structural link is marriage. The man holds the formal authority vested in men, and the woman holds the right to confer matriline membership by virtue of a relationship with her; when a marriage takes place, the two principles intertwine. When a man marries in—and, as I have mentioned, matrilocal residence is the rule—the third principle, that of senior-junior relationships, becomes important, and the new son-in-law must defer to the authority of his seniors. When Father Good married Mother Celestial, he moved to her courtyard and paid a token sum to her ancestral spirits, so that he would be a member of the group protected by them. This is the single crucial element in the marriage ceremony. He placed himself under the authority of Mother Celestial's father, Grandfather Ten Thousand. He gave his name, Plenitude, to Mother Celestial, as required by the national law of 1916; before that law took effect, Northern Thai peasants did not have surnames. His present position as head of the family is the result of his having come into his affinal inheritance when Grandfather Ten Thousand, his father-in-law, died, a mere two years ago. For all the previous years of his marriage, Father Good was a subordinate.

As far as the future of the courtyard is concerned, New Dawn, the youngest daughter who will almost certainly inherit the house, will confer upon her future husband the matriline membership which will give him the right to exercise his authority, and New Dawn's future husband will inherit the position of head of the household from Father Good. Who this man, of such importance to the future of the family, may be is left to the vicissitudes of New Dawn's experiences with courtship. Thus the process of courtship is of very great importance to the structure of family life. It is important to note that Keen, the only son, who was born into the courtyard, can expect no form of inherited authority from the family of his birth. He can only become head of a household when he has married. He will be protected by his wife's family spirits. He will inherit authority in his new family from his father-in-law, and by virtue of his relationship with his wife.

In a system like this, the wife is in a most important position. Her husband's status in the family is conferred by her. She has the job of mediating between her husband and her father, who are separated from one another by an avoidance taboo. She is the connecting link, bound to her father by one sort of love, and to her husband by another. There is a great deal of mediating to do, since the father and the husband have interests which are frequently opposed to one another. The son-in-law, like any heir, is eager to take control, and the father-in-law is reluctant to relinquish it. There is no relationship of long standing, as there would be between father and son, to ease the conflict, since the son-in-law joins the family when the daughter is an adult, and by her choice. (Parents may make suggestions and apply pressure, but it is the custom for a man and a woman to choose one another, and marry for love.) The effect of all this is to give a woman an important voice in the management of family life, a position of power which comes from her place in the structure of the family. Thus, the specific kind of structure has the effect of increasing the importance of women, even though formal authority is vested in men. However, the rule of respect for seniors tends to reinforce the position of the husband.

Father Good's status as head of the family is reinforced by his being the oldest: Mother Celestial's secondary position as the woman is reinforced because she is junior to her husband.

(People in Chiangmai Village always laugh at a couple where the wife is older, and it happens very rarely, since it creates an internal contradiction in the relationship between husband and wife.) Children are supposed to treat their parents with a special sort of intimate deference, and they almost always do. Among the children, older siblings are respectfully addressed as Older Sister, if female, or Older Brother, if male, along with their names. Younger siblings are addressed by their names alone. Older siblings are obligated to take care of younger ones. Younger siblings are obligated to help older siblings as best they can. As a result, the older have very different experiences of family life from the younger. Older Sister Blessing remembers a childhood spent mostly in baby-sitting. New Dawn remembers a childhood during which she was constantly at other people's beck and call, and rarely required to take responsibility. The only partial exception to the rule of respect to seniors is in the treatment of people who are so old that they can no longer take responsibility for others. All of the Plenitudes know that they must take care of Grandmother Worth, and that she is unable to take care of them. This makes a difference in the way she is treated: she is cared for in accordance with her diminished capabilities, and the Plenitudes do not defer to her quite as they would if she were more vigorous.

The Plenitude family as it now exists is based on the marriage relationship between Father Good and Mother Celestial. Marriage in Chiangmai Village is a most undemonstrative relationship. The greatest display of affection ever seen between Father Good and Mother Celestial is when she gives him a cigarette she has rolled using the tobacco he prefers. Village ideas about human relationships put a married couple in a curious position. In Chiangmai Village the desire to please others is mocked. Human commitments to people outside of one's own family are concealed for fear of betrayal, rejection, and merciless teasing. Yet it is just such a relationship, in which two unrelated people form a permanent commitment to one another, which is a prerequisite for the working of the social system. Paradoxically, all the emotional factors which went into the forming of the bond between a husband and wife are kept hidden after their marriage, although the bond itself is such an important element of the social structure. As a result, a proper couple like Father Good and Mother Celestial are willing to expose very little of their feelings for one another. Yet their marriage has lasted more than thirty-six years, they still make occasional small gestures of mutual affection, and they are rarely heard to quarrel, even at night, when muffled voices sometimes argue behind the thin wooden or bamboo walls of the houses of the village. The childrens' expectations about the nature of a marriage may give some clues to the quality of their parents' relationship. The children expect that an angry wife will threaten to break up a marriage, but that gentle placating words will make her change her mind; that women lay traps to test men; that men are likely to deceive women in pursuit of their own pleasures; that women make most of the important decisions in a family; and that a woman can expect a warm and positive response from a friend if she criticizes the friend's husband. All of these expectations point, by implication, to sources of strain which are not revealed. Father Good and Mother Celestial try to keep the human dynamics of their relationship cloaked.

Forming a marriage is a delicate and complex process, which is of absorbing interest to everyone in the village. It is of particular interest to the Plenitude children, who are at the age when they must find spouses of their own. In Chiangmai Village young people do not like to make themselves vulnerable by entering into a new relationship which requires trust. They are afraid of being rejected, or used, or embarrassed by gossip, and there is very little privacy in the village. The customs of courtship provide ways of easing these fears. In the early stages of courtship, a young man has the support of his peer group, and the young woman of her parents and sisters. The conversations of courtship are carried on in a formal pattern which preserves social ambiguity so that no one is embarrassed by the appearance of being committed to another. The custom is for groups of young men who are friends to form courting groups, and baj ʔɛw, or "go around" together in the evening, visiting at houses where attractive young women are known to live. Keen has been going around to visit young women for almost ten years now, with a group of his closest friends. The young women wait at home, nicely dressed, and with the door open as a sign that callers are welcome.

Nowadays the young men who come to visit at the Plenitude courtyard are mostly interested in New Dawn and Holy Day. Some evenings, the young men begin to arrive even before New Dawn (who, as youngest, must let her seniors bathe first) has finished in the bathing enclosure. Then there is banter in the courtyard, interspersed with the sloshing of water behind the brick walls, until New Dawn emerges fully dressed in clean clothes, and the party moves upstairs. Or if there is some form of work going on under the house, like separating garlic cloves for planting, the young people help with that, and work while they talk. New Dawn laughs and flirts, but Holy Day is very shy. Holy Day sits quietly in her beautiful green skirt with the delicate zigzag pattern. She listens to the talk, and occasionally puts in a word. Sometimes the conversation is of the ordinary sort, but sometimes it is the special formal conversation of courtship, ʔûu baw, ʔûu saw, "the talk of young men, the talk of young women," a kind of verbal game using rhymes and playing with words. Without practice it is difficult to tell when the conversation becomes a formal game and when it does not, and even with practice it is still difficult, because of the element of calculated ambiguity. When the conversation becomes formal and uses rhymes, the key to the game is answering a conventional question in terms that rhyme with words expressing one's true feelings. For example, if such a conversation were to take place in English, a young man might ask a young woman what she had for dinner. She might love him, and answer, "Roast dove," or she might feel shy, and answer, "Cream cheese on rye." Or she might not want to play, and tell him what she really had.

The following is a sample conversation:

> A group of young men enters the courtyard. A young woman calls down from above.

YOUNG WOMAN: Please come upstairs, why don't you?

YOUNG MAN: That's all right, I'll stay down here a minute. I feel too hot.

> (The word "hot" refers both to temperature and to lust.)

> The young men come upstairs. The one most interested in the young woman talks to her.

YOUNG WOMAN: Have you come to visit me?

YOUNG MAN: Yes, I have.

YOUNG WOMAN: How many of you are there?

YOUNG MAN: Oh, two or three.

YOUNG WOMAN: What did you have for supper at your house?

> (This question, along with "Where are you going?" is a standard greeting.)

YOUNG MAN: Green vegetable curry with sauce made in a mortar and pestle.

(He is complimenting the girl. What he really says is:

> *Keŋ phak láʔ sàj njaa taam.*

This sounds like:

> *maa paʔ saw tîi nîi ŋam taa,*

which means, "I've come to see a girl with beautiful eyes.")

The young man has other punning phrases at his disposal. If he wants to make sure that the girl won't deceive him, he may say:

> *keng pratuu bâan saj can lúʔ*

which means curried front door seasoned with kitchen drain. The words he uses suggest:

> *maa ʔɛw tîi bâan nîi capaj cúʔ nŷy.*

105

This means, "I've come courting to this house, and please don't deceive me."

YOUNG MAN (continues): What did you have for supper here?

YOUNG WOMAN: I had pepper sauce.

(She is saying two things, first that she is hot-tempered like peppers, and second, that she wants him to go home—the word for pepper is *phik,* and the word for go home is *phík.*)

If she is feeling ferocious, she can say she had *keŋ jûak,* which is curried vegetable, and that will remind the young man of the word *sûak,* which means ferocious.

If she loves him, she can say she had curried *fak* plant; *fak* rhymes with *hak,* which means love.

If she is very angry she may say she had curried mustard greens, *phakaad.* That will remind him of *phat khɔ̌ɔ,* which means cut your throat.

YOUNG WOMAN (continuing conversation): Have you transplanted rice yet at your house?

YOUNG MAN: No, we haven't. I've come looking for someone to help us.

YOUNG WOMAN: Where are you looking?

YOUNG MAN: Right here in Chiangmai Village.

YOUNG WOMAN: There are a lot of houses in Chiangmai Village. Which one you might be meaning, I don't know.

YOUNG MAN: I want the person I'm talking to right now. Can you come?

YOUNG WOMAN: Oh, you don't really mean it.

YOUNG MAN: I do mean it, and if you go I will be very grateful.

(They both know that she would be displaying an improperly forward interest in him if she came; it is a foregone conclusion that she won't.)

YOUNG WOMAN: I'm afraid that if I went to help you plant, your rice crop wouldn't be nice this year.

YOUNG MAN: If you planted it, it would be the nicest it's ever been.

(If the young couple are not previously acquainted, they may go on like this:)

106

YOUNG WOMAN: We've been talking together for a long time already, and I don't know your name. Excuse me, what is it?

YOUNG MAN: My name isn't beautiful. I couldn't possibly tell you.

YOUNG WOMAN: I don't mind if it isn't beautiful. If you would tell me, I would be very glad to hear.

YOUNG MAN: My name is *Khen.*

(Khen means "leftovers".)

YOUNG WOMAN: Do you have a place to stay over at?

(She is making a pun, because the word for leftovers is the same as the word for stay over.)

YOUNG MAN: No, I don't have any place to stay over, and if you have any room left over, I'd like to stay over at this house. What people come courting at this house?

YOUNG WOMAN: There isn't anyone who comes courting here.

(Because of propriety, she has to say this, even if she has many boyfriends.)

YOUNG MAN: If you really don't have anyone coming courting, I'd like to come as a regular thing, if I may.

YOUNG WOMAN: If you aren't angry at this household, you can certainly come.

YOUNG MAN: I'm afraid you have a boyfriend already. If you do, please tell me, and I won't come around and bother you again.

YOUNG WOMAN: I don't have a boyfriend; if I did have, I would surely tell you. I really, really don't.

YOUNG MAN: If you really don't, I'll come again soon.

YOUNG WOMAN: I'm afraid *you* have a girlfriend already.

YOUNG MAN: No, I don't; if I did, what would I come courting to this house for?

YOUNG WOMAN: You're just saying what you feel at this particular moment.

YOUNG MAN: Let me come courting regularly, and you'll see for yourself.

YOUNG WOMAN: If you really come I'm not afraid, but I'm afraid you're only kidding.

All the examples come from experience. The word games in the conversation, as well as being entertaining, provide a merciful ambiguity in the relationship between the young man and the young woman. If the young woman decides that she doesn't love the young man after all, she can comfort herself with the thought that she merely said she had curried *bafak* for supper, which might have been the literal truth. The young man knows that the young woman is acting with propriety when she denies that anyone else visits her; he is aware that she is following social form, and he doesn't *expect* the literal truth. Nothing that has been said is binding. Both parties have expressed distrust: partly for the pleasure of being reassured, no doubt, yet both know that they cannot trust the reassurances. A couple's feelings for one another take shape behind a social smoke screen. To outsiders, to the gossiping village as a whole, to one's self, even, it is always possible to deny that an involvement exists at all.

There is another factor which contributes to the distrustfulness of courtship in Chiangmai Village and this is the double standard of sexual behavior. The young men hope that the banter of courtship will lead to something more, short of marriage, since they gain status if their peers believe that they have seduced many women. But a young woman embarrasses her parents and loses her reputation (the term used means "to be spoiled by comparison") if people hear that she has slept with a young man. Her chances of marriage are likely to be reduced. Also, premarital sex offends the protective spirits of the young woman's family. The spirits insist on formal, complete, and prompt information whenever a person under their protection changes status or forms a new relationship. The young woman must arrange to placate the spirits or else risk their hostile intervention. In general, the young women try, in accordance with propriety, to resist the advances of the young men.

All of the Plenitude children have been impeded in the process of courtship and the attempt to find a husband or wife. Older Sister Clear and Older Sister Fine Qualities both married after years of concerted opposition by Father Good and Mother Celestial. Their husbands were loyal and determined suitors, and suffered inconvenience, criticism, and unkindness. Older Sister Clear was allowed to marry only after she was pregnant, and Older Brother Eye courted her honorably for years before that happened. Mother Celestial never liked Older Sister Fine Qualities' husband, and even at Older Sister Fine Qualities' death in childbirth, she was still not reconciled to the marriage. Of the other seven children, only Spin Out Gold has found a lover who is loyal and determined enough, and their affection for one another has already been severely tested. Spin Out Gold's boyfriend runs a barbershop in a leaf-roofed shelter along the road from the temple. He and Spin Out Gold agreed to get married, and he began the formal process by asking for his parents' agreement. His parents said they would be happy to agree to the marriage. The next step for them was to visit Father Good and Mother Celestial and to ask for Spin Out Gold as their son's wife. This visit was not a success. Father Good and Mother Celestial were cold and unfriendly. They intimated that the young man was too poor to be a good match for Spin Out Gold. The young man's parents were hurt. They replied that Spin Out Gold wasn't a good match either, since she is not beautiful, and her lameness means that she works slowly, so that everyone else has more to do. Then both sets of parents were angry and distressed, and the marriage seemed to be broken off. However, Spin Out Gold and her boyfriend agreed that they still loved one another and wished to marry. Spin Out Gold is working hard to save money so that they need ask nothing from Father Good and Mother Celestial, and she hopes to marry soon.

The other six children have not been able to form lasting relationships. Some village gossips say that Mother Celestial is raising a family of old maids. Full of Fineness, the daughter of the village head, who is also New Dawn's good friend, thinks that if only they would all get married, everyone would be much happier, and that is probably true. But in every case, courtships have failed—because of something in the hearts of the Plenitude children, or parental interference, or lack of perseverence by suitors, or even fate, since it is not always possible for everyone to find a compatible mate in the natural course of events. Older Sister Blessing says that she doesn't think of marriage any more. She has recently turned down an offer from a widower with children. Moonlight has been courted by many attractive people, but in every case the courtship has not succeeded. One young man told her that she was his only girlfriend, but left her to marry another girl he had been secretly courting at the same time. Another man, whom Moonlight had begun to love, heard that her parents wouldn't let her marry a man who wasn't rich. He stopped courting her for fear of their opposition. Now he lives in the nearby village of Four Cornered Pond with a wife and three children. A third courtship came very close to ending in marriage; the man was from central Thailand, and had a truck, which made him both exotic and wealthy. Mother Celestial liked this man. The village gossips, who say that she interferes with her childrens' marriages because she wants richer spouses for them, whispered unkindly that she was delighted to have a truck for a son-in-law. However, Grandfather Ten Thousand had the marriage stopped at the last moment, on the grounds that the Plenitudes knew nothing of the young man beyond his present situation. They would be sending Moonlight into potentially dangerous circumstances far from home, where they would not be able to help her. As things worked out, Grandfather Ten Thousand's instinct was correct. The man had a wife already, and Moonlight would have had to take the position of minor wife, to which she is unsuited by pride, temperament, and her desire to be an exemplar of the conventions. Perhaps the saddest of Moonlight's disappointments

was a young man who came back to visit her after an absence
of two years. He had been away studying so that he could
manage a government health post to be set up in Pond's Edge
(a neighboring village) and Moonlight had thought he must
have forgotten her. This young man rode into the courtyard
on his Vespa, and the sadness and tension which are visible
on Moonlight's face in repose lifted suddenly, to be replaced
with pleasure and delight. She looked young and beautiful
again, at least to me. The young man visited with Moonlight
and went with her to a temple fair in the evening. They seemed
to be having a very good time in one another's company. The
next day Moonlight said that he had proposed to her, and she
had answered that she thought she would like to marry him,
although she wasn't certain. She had tested him to make sure
he didn't drink too heavily, and he had refused her offers of
more rice wine. And his professions of love must have sounded
very sincere and fervent indeed, to convince Moonlight, who
does not trust easily, that he really meant to marry her. But
the days went by, and he never came back. Gradually the joy
faded from Moonlight's face, and things were as they had been
before. Moonlight tries to maintain a proud front, but once
she cried, and said that she had never married because she
had never loved anyone, ever. Then she said that she was
afraid: she didn't want things to happen to her that happen to
people who have bad luck. After that she didn't mention the
young man on the Vespa again, even obliquely.

Keen in his many years of courting, has never found a young
woman he wants to marry, although he has visited steadily at
several houses. He enjoys the process of courtship: dressing in
good clothes, riding a motorcycle, and going around with his
peer group, which is more important to him than any young
woman has been. Keen acts as if courtship were an end in
itself, rather than a means. Keen remains, at least partly by
choice, at home with his parents. His bachelorhood has caused
comment in the village. Full of Fineness, the daughter of the
village head, says that Keen has never been able to find a

111

young woman as rich and as pretty as he wants. Full of Fineness adds that if such an eligible young woman did exist, she might want to marry someone younger and richer than Keen.

The two youngest daughters, Holy Day and New Dawn, are still at the beginning of their courting. Perhaps they will be luckier than the others. However, Holy Day's speech defect makes her less attractive, and fewer young men single her out. New Dawn is courted by a young man of Pond's Edge, but he is very poor, and he is thinking of staying away for fear that Father Good and Mother Celestial will forbid him to marry her. New Dawn loves him, and he loves her, or so they both tell one another. However, New Dawn has also said that she considers herself too young to marry. New Dawn's boyfriend is worried, and with reason.

As long as they remain unmarried and live in the courtyard, the younger Plenitudes continue to follow the well-worn paths of family relationships which were mapped out years ago. The recent history of the Plenitude family has been dominated by the powerful personality of Grandfather Ten Thousand. It was he who made his family into a successful and prosperous rice growing enterprise. At the same time he rose to eminence in village politics. Yet he was a disappointed man. He shared with his wife the sorrow of losing four of their five children in infancy. He had wished for a son, but the child who survived was a daughter. He was a man of bitter and punishing rages, which Grandmother Worth would try ineffectually to quell by putting her hand on his arm, and saying gently, "Oh, Ten Thousand, Ten Thousand." Because of his strength and force of character, all of the Plenitudes have spent most of their lives as juniors, following orders and receiving protection, but having very little discretion over their own welfare. Father Good was a subordinate for more than thirty years. It is not surprising that his authority lacks the assurance which practice would have given it, or that he treats Older Sister Clear's husband, Older Brother Eye, as he himself was treated. Father

Good's own son, Keen, was the apple of Grandfather Ten Thousand's eye, and the two of them had a relationship which Father Good could not participate in. Keen knew that he could always appeal successfully from the authority of his father to the authority of his grandfather. Grandfather Ten Thousand's influence affected Father Good's relationship with Mother Celestial also. Mother Celestial is a strong woman, and her opinions were often supported by Grandfather Ten Thousand. Father Good bore the burdens of the role of son-in-law, and also the effects of Grandfather Ten Thousand's idiosyncracies.

Grandfather Ten Thousand had an intense influence on Mother Celestial's behavior, as child, wife, and mother. Since Mother Celestial was the only child of a couple who had lost many children, she was most precious to her father. He often restricted her liberty in trying to keep her safe. Mother Celestial tells how he was afraid to let her ride a bicycle like everyone else, and she finally had to learn by riding around the courtyard in circles at the end of a rope. When Mother Celestial became a mother, Grandfather Ten Thousand continued to tell her what to do. When Keen was born, Grandfather Ten Thousand cherished him in the same encircling way that he had cherished Mother Celestial herself. He was angry at Mother Celestial if she allowed Keen to be unhappy, and he insisted that she give up everything which took her away from the courtyard. He even hired another woman so that Mother Celestial wouldn't have to do the marketing. This meant that Mother Celestial had to lead an extremely restricted life. Although she was proud of Keen, at the same time she was jealous of her father's love for him. She makes it clear that her love for her father was diluted with resentment because he kept her so confined.

As far as the Plenitude children other than Keen were concerned, Grandfather Ten Thousand's rages and demonstrations of affection were the source of emotions which still

113

simmer and seethe. Holy Day's timidity was increased by Grandfather Ten Thousand, who once beat her for being gone too long gathering edible algae. She says that he was a man who exuded anger. Grandfather Ten Thousand's open delight in Keen embittered Keen's sisters. Moonlight says, "Keen always had everything he wanted, because he was a little plump boy." Without Grandfather Ten Thousand, the Plenitudes would not be the way they are, or feel the way they do about one another, and the two years since his death have not freed them from him.

6

Encounters with Spirits

There are many different kinds of spirits in Chiangmai Village. Spirits populate the paths, gardens, fields, and houses of the village in a shadowy society: a society which mirrors that of human beings in certain important respects. Some of the spirits are the spirits which belong to matrilines. What they are and what they do afford indications of the way matrilines are organized, and what values matrilines enforce, thus clarifying important aspects of social structure. All spirits, whether they are the spirits of groups, the spirits of places, deceptive spirits, or possessing spirits, are believed to behave according to a pattern which casts light on expectations, fears, and beliefs about other people. The spirits elucidate the nature of human relationships in the village, as well as social structure.

The spirits which belong to the Plenitudes' matriline inhabit the northern corner of the eastern bedroom, next to Grandmother Worth's bed. They are continuously present, in their disembodied way. They are the spirits of former members of the matriline, both male and female. It must be remembered that the male spirits are affines, the female ones consanguines. Thus, the spirits include both of Grandmother Worth's parents, her mother's parents (but not her father's parents, who would have belonged to a different group), her mother's mother's parents, and so on. The spirit of Grandmother Worth's mother's brother, if she had had one, would not be included, because he would have joined the spirit group of his wife. Only if he remained unmarried would he retain membership in his natal spirit group. The spirits are not remembered by name, as individuals, but as an undifferentiated group, and records of the names of spirits of the matriline are not kept.

Everyone who lives in the courtyard is protected by the spirits, since they are all members of the same matriline. All of them were born into it, except Father Good, and Older Brother Eye, who became members at marriage. Keen is a member now, but if he marries he will no longer belong, because he will join his wife's group instead, and his children will not belong.

The spirits which protect the Plenitudes' matriline live in their house because it is the "old-established" house of the lineage. The spirits stay in the same house for generation after generation. Houses are inherited by whichever child stays to care for the parents in their old age, and this is usually the youngest daughter. An "old-established" house tends to pass from youngest daughter to youngest daughter, while other children move away to houses of their own. The Plenitudes' house came from Grandmother Worth's mother, who was a younger daughter, through Grandmother Worth, who was an only child, to Mother Celestial, also an only child. All the descendants of older daughters live in houses established after the original installation of the spirits in what is now the Plenitudes' house, hence their houses are not called "old-established," but the spirits still protect them. The spirits offer a conditional protection to the people under their care: they protect if they are politely treated, receive offerings, and are formally informed of every important family event or change of status of a family member.

Like living relatives, they are offended if they discover that they were the last to know anything of interest or importance. Then they withdraw their protection and cause the offender to fall ill. The spirits are greatly concerned with the sexual behavior of daughters of the matriline. If a young woman sleeps with a man, she must tell her mother, so that a propitiatory offering can be made to the spirits. If the young woman is too shy to tell her mother, the spirits are angry, and the mother will fall ill. Then, if a spirit medium is called in to hold a curing ceremony, the reason for the illness will be made public in the course of the ceremony. This would be most humiliating to the daughter. Thus the spirits enforce the value of premarital chastity for women.

When a couple marries, the new husband has to give a sum of money to propitiate his wife's matrilineal spirits. This is the crucial element of the marriage formalities, and it is possible to be married without any other ceremony. Father Good and Mother Celestial were married in this way—Father Good simply made the offerings and moved in. If a man and woman who are members of the same matriline marry one another, the spirits are angry, and punish them with ill health, madness, and death. There are two couples in Chiangmai Village whose marriages violate the spirits' scrupulous incest rules; they have suffered from ill health, and their money has gone for propitiation ceremonies.

Once a year the ancestral spirits are honored by a special ceremony, to which every household in the matriline contributes. The ceremony takes place in the ninth month of the lunar calendar, on the tenth day of that part of the month in which the moon wanes. This usually occurs in June. The ceremony is held at the "old-established house" where the spirits live, and it is conducted by an hereditary mistress of ceremonies. The mistress of ceremonies is a senior woman in the group of matriline members. Usually her mother held the

117

position before her. For the Plenitudes' matriline, the mistress of ceremonies is Grandmother Heart's Content, who lives at the south end of the village near the cremation ground. Grandmother Heart's Content's mother was the oldest sister of Grandmother Worth's mother. Grandmother Heart's Content herself was the second daughter, not the oldest. Grandmother Heart's Content comes to the Plenitudes' house, offers food to the spirits, and prays for protection in the coming year. She is on friendly terms with the spirits. She has a method for finding out whether they have had all the food they want before the plates are distributed among the living: she picks a pinch of milled rice from one of the offering plates, and counts the number of grains. If the number is even, she knows that the spirits are satisfied, but if it is odd, she leaves the food before them for ten or fifteen minutes more and then tries again. She keeps trying until she draws an even number of grains.

The kinds of spirits other than matriline spirits which the Plenitudes have encountered have all been frightening and malevolent. The Plenitudes have seen deceiving spirits which take the form of people or animals, they have been attacked as trespassers by spirits which dwell in trees and paths, and they have been frightened in their own house by a restless spirit lately dead, the spirit of Older Sister Fine Qualities.

Mother Celestial and New Dawn are the ones who have encountered spirits in deceptive forms. Mother Celestial saw a spirit dog as she crossed a field in the early morning, and a spirit in the form of a child in a tree as she went to visit in another village. New Dawn saw a spirit which had taken the shape of a cat. People can penetrate a spirit's intention to deceive by an intuitive sense that they are confronted with something unnatural. Also, deceiving spirits always vanish eventually, unlike humans who try deceptive tricks in love or business. A cynical village proverb says,

phǐi lɔɔg njang mii wan hǎj
khon bɔɔ tǎaj
maa lɔɔg kan dâj.

This means something like,

> Deceiving ghosts of those who've died will ultimately
> disappear
> While people who are still alive deceive each other
> far and near.

The proverb explicitly compares the deceptiveness of spirits with the deceptiveness of humans; the latter are, if anything, worse. The expectation of being tricked and deceived in relationships, which emerges so clearly in the context of courtship, is demonstrated again in attitudes toward spirits.

Keen was actually stricken with a paralyzing illness by a malevolent spirit. This was an invisible spirit living in a tree. Father Good had purchased the tree for firewood, and Keen went with several of his sisters to cut it down and bind the wood into bundles. Keen had the man's job of climbing the tree and doing the cutting, and Moonlight and Older Sister Blessing had the woman's part, binding the wood into bundles. Together they carried the wood home in the evening. Then Keen felt ill, and lay on his bed without moving. He called for his parents in the night, but they thought he was drunk, and wouldn't come to him. After that he ceased to speak as well as to move. He lay silent and immobile for a day and a night, and when he showed no signs of recovery, Father Good and Mother Celestial were frightened. They sent for a man named Father Eye, whom they liked and respected, and who has the spiritual strength to deal with supernaturally caused illnesses. Father Eye listened to their story, and then he said that Keen was being attacked by the spirit which had inhabited the tree. He thought that the spirit could probably be appeased by an offering of chicken and rice wine. Father Good got some rice

119

wine and a chicken, and taking Father Eye with him, went to the place where the tree had been. They built a little platform as a sort of altar and offered up the chicken and the rice wine. Soon after they returned home, Keen began to recover, and by the next day, he was quite well. One never knows when one is offending a spirit, and the punishment is harsh, but the spirits will usually accept an offering and an apology.

Among the most dangerous spirits are the spirits of those who have died unfulfilled. Older Sister Fine Qualities, the Plenitude daughter who was younger than Older Sister Blessing and older than Moonlight, died in such a sorrowful and thwarted way that her spirit had to be appeased with special offerings. Older Sister Fine Qualities was both pretty and popular when she was alive, and she married a young man who had a barber shop in the nearby market village of Road's Entrance. After a time she became pregnant, and when it was time to give birth, she came back to her parents' house, so that her mother and sisters could take care of her. She had a very difficult labor, and after two days of it, they finally took her to the hospital. There she labored another day and gave birth to twin sons who died when they were a few minutes old. Then Older Sister Fine Qualities died of a blood clot in the brain. Her body was taken to a cremating ground near the hospital in a special ambulance, because no taxi would risk being haunted by so malevolent a spirit, and she was hurriedly cremated there, rather than at the village cremating ground. Mother Celestial railed against Older Sister Fine Qualities' husband in her sorrow, and said if it weren't for him, she would still have her daughter. Older Sister Fine Qualities' husband was very much afraid that her spirit would return to harm him. He entered a monastery for several months to make merit for the spirit and be protected from it by religious power. The Plenitudes were as frightened as he was. They knew that Older Sister Fine Qualities had been a sociable, company-loving person while she was alive, and they inferred that she would seek company after death. They decided to consult a medium who could tell them how to appease Older Sister Fine Qualities' spirit. Mother Celestial heard of a spirit medium of considerable reputation who lived in a village some miles north of Chiengmai, and the whole family went to consult her. Tender Gold, who lives next door, and the wife of Father Seeker, who is a near neighbor and shares the same matriline spirits, went with them.

When they arrived at the village and found the spirit medium, she agreed to hold a seance for them. She began by proving to them that her powers were real. She did this by pointing out people in the group and telling what relation each one was to Older Sister Fine Qualities, although she had never seen them before and had no way of knowing about the family. She told each of them details of their own lives that she would have had to know by magic rather than by report or observation. Then she invited Older Sister Fine Qualities' spirit to enter her, and went into a trance. She spoke to the family with the voice of Older Sister Fine Qualities. Older Sister Fine Qualities said that she was suffering for lack of clothes and shoes and blankets. She asked them to hold the special ceremony in which these things are donated to the temple, so that the priest serves as the living intermediary who accepts gifts on behalf of the dead. Older Sister Fine Qualities said that she had come to the house once in search of clothes, but that if the ceremony were held for her, she would not come back again. As Holy Day listened to the spirit medium talking in Older Sister Fine Qualities' voice, she suddenly remembered a night shortly after Older Sister Fine Qualities' death, when she had lain awake listening, and had heard a noise like a mouse in the clothing cupboards. She was sure that that must have been the time Older Sister Fine Qualities came back. Everyone was quite excited, and agreed with Holy Day.

Then the spirit medium explained why Older Sister Fine Qualities had died. She had been killed by a spirit, the spirit

121

of a man who had died in a traffic accident near Older Sister Fine Qualities' house in Road's Entrance. Bitterness and agony of mind had filled this spirit, because it had died before its time, and it had sought a victim.

The Plenitudes returned from the seance feeling somewhat reassured. They knew the reason for Older Sister Fine Qualities' death, and they knew what they could do to make her more comfortable. They held the ceremony and offered the clothes and bedding Older Sister Fine Qualities had asked for. The ceremony was a success, in the sense that the spirit of Older Sister Fine Qualities did not return to haunt the house, but people do not know where they stand with spirits any more than they do with fellow human beings. The Plenitudes are afraid Older Sister Fine Qualities might return anyway; it would be frightening if she did.

Spirits in the village share many of the harshest characteristics of people. They turn their anger on those who have done them no harm. They insist on due respect and formality, and an oversight or failure in politeness fills them with rage. They bear grudges, and they insist on knowing people's most intimate business. They are not to be trusted, they are treacherous, their motives are dark, and they take pleasure in deceiving. This is what the people of Chiangmai Village expect and fear from others, whether living or dead.

Conclusion

I have dealt with two interrelated questions in this book.

First, what is the structure of a Northern Thai family? This question emerges from a body of anthropological literature which suggests that family life in Thailand is formless or loosely structured. I have shown that this is not the case. Instead, Northern Thai family structure can be understood as a system in which lineality is traced through women, rather than men, and authority is passed on affinally, from father-in-law to son-in-law, by virtue of their relationships to the line of women. This new type of family system, a novel recombination of familiar elements—sex, lineality, affinality, and the inheritance of authority—is not previously reported in the literature. The key factor in understanding the system is the recognition of the structural importance of women; without that, the system is unintelligible.

Second, how do individuals experience social structure in the context of the family? I have dealt with this in two ways: by showing the demands structure places on different family members, and by showing how each individual brings his or her idiosyncracies to the structural context and takes away a unique and utterly personal experience of life. The description

123

and analysis of social structure should not be dehumanized and made lifeless by omitting any mention of individual experience.

I have explained and resolved a system which appeared formless and inchoate, and shown some of the effects of the system on the human beings who must live within it. At the same time, I have tried to give a glimpse into another cultural world.

Bibliography

Davis, Richard
  1974 "Tolerance and Intolerance of Ambiguity in Northern Thai Myth and Ritual," *Ethnology* XIII:7-24.

de Young, John
  1955 *Village Life in Modern Thailand.* Berkeley and Los Angeles: University of California Press.

Embree, John F.
  1950 "Thailand—A Loosely Structured Social System," *American Anthropologist* 52: 181-193.

Evers, Hans-Dieter
  1969 "Models of Social Systems: Loosely and Tightly Structured." In *Loosely Structured Social Systems: Thailand in Comparative Perspective,* edited by Hans-Dieter Evers. New Haven: Yale University Southeast Asia Cultural Report Series, No. 17.

Geertz, Hildred
  1961 *The Javanese Family: A Study of Kinship and Social Organization.* New York: Free Press.

Haas, Mary R.
  1967 *Thai-English Student's Dictionary.* Stanford: Stanford University Press.

Kaufman, Howard Keva
  1960 *Bangkhuad: A Community Study in Thailand.* Monograph No. 10 of the Association for Asian Studies. Locust Valley, N.Y.: J. J. Augustin, Inc.

Kingshill, Konrad
  1965 *Ku Daeng—The Red Tomb.* Bangkok: Bangkok Christian College. (First edition, 1960.)

Lévi-Strauss, Claude
  1953 "Social Structure." In *Anthropology Today,* edited by A. L. Kroeber. Chicago. University of Chicago Press.

125

Mizuno, Koichi
  1971   *Social System of Don Daeng Village: A Community Study in Northeast Thailand.* Mimeographed. Kyoto, Japan: Discussion Papers Nos. 12–22 of the Center for Southeast Asian Studies.

Moerman, Michael
  1966   "Ban Ping's Temple: The Center of a Loosely Structured Society." In *Anthropological Studies in Theravada Buddhism,* edited by Manning Nash. New Haven: Yale University Southeast Asia Cultural Report Series, No. 13.

Mulder, J. A. Niels
  1969   "Origin, Development, and Use of the Concept of 'Loose Structure' in the Literature about Thailand: An Evaluation." In *Loosely Structured Social Systems: Thailand in Comparative Perspective,* edited by Hans-Dieter Evers. New Haven: Yale University Southeast Asia Cultural Report Series, No. 17.

Phillips, Herbert P.
  1965   *Thai Peasant Personality: The Patterning of Interpersonal Behavior in the Village of Bang Chan.* Berkeley and Los Angeles: University of California Press.

Piker, Steven
  1969   " 'Loose Structure' and the Analysis of Thai Social Organization." In *Loosely Structured Social Systems: Thailand in Comparative Perspective,* edited by Hans-Dieter Evers. New Haven: Yale University Southeast Asia Cultural Report Series, No. 17.

Sharp, Lauriston, et al.
  1953   *Siamese Rice Village: A Preliminary Study of Bang Chan, 1948– 1949.* Bangkok: Cornell Research Center.

Smith, Harvey, et al.
  1968   *Area Handbook for Thailand.* Washington, D. C.: U. S. Government Printing Office.

Solien de Gonzales, Nancie
  1965   "The Consanguineal Household and Matrifocality," *American Anthropologist,* 67:1541–49.

Tambiah, S. J.
  1966   "Review of *Thai Peasant Personality* by Herbert P. Phillips," *Man,* 1:424.
  1970   *Buddhism and the Spirit Cults in North-east Thailand.* Cambridge: Cambridge University Press.

Turton, Andrew
  1972   "Matrilineal Descent Groups and Spirit Cults of the Thai-Yuan in Northern Thailand." *Journal of the Siam Society,* 60:217–256.

Wijeyewardene, Gehan
   1967   "Some Aspects of Rural Life in Thailand." In *Thailand: Social and Economic Studies in Development,* edited by T. H. Silcock. Durham: Duke University Press.

Index

Address, terms of: and age, 33; among children, 102; for married people, 30

Affines, and economic cooperation, 12. *See also* Male affines

Age: deference and responsibility relative to, 8, 99, 102; differences between husband and wife, 101–102; and education, 50, 96; and location of beds, 38, 39; and orders to the youngest family member, 39, 48, 102; and terms of address, 33, 102. *See also* Old people; Senior-junior relationships; Youngest daughter

Agricultural labor exchange groups: basis of, 58–60; on an individual level, 58, 65; as a structural tie, 90

Amyot, Jacques, 12

Ancestral spirits. *See* Matrilineal ancestral spirits

Anthropological research: methods of author, 2, 21–22; about the Thai family structure, 4–20, 123

Anthropologists' house, 27, 49

Anthropology: as "history" or "thick description," 1; mechanical models in, 8; statistical models in, 8, 9

Authority: of father, 54–55, 60, 99–100, 101, 112–113; of grandfather, 30, 39, 100, 112–113; inherited affinally by men from father-in-law, 20, 55, 100–101, 123; limits to, 14; of men, 99–101

Avoidance taboo: between son-in-law and father-in-law, 55, 101; between son-in-law and parents-in-law, 50

Ban Ping, Thailand, kinship in, 9

Banana leaves, uses for, 74, 94

Bang Chan, Thailand: extended family households in, 12; neolocal residence patterns in, 5; psychological study in, 7–8

Bangkhuad, Thailand: family responsibility in, 7; household family in, 6

Bathing, 81, 104

Beds, positions and locations of, 36, 38–39, 48

Begging, 51, 92

Bilateral kinship, 14; and agricultural cooperation, 58–59

Blanchard, Wendell, 10

Breakfast meal, 77, 78

Bright Eyes, as visitor to the courtyard, 50–51

Brothers-in-law, 19

Buddha image, in main house, 34

Buddhism: cultural ties of with Chiang-mai Village, 83; and eating meat, 73; and food donated to the temple, 92; ideal of detachment in, 96; lenten season of, 84. *See also* Temple

Cash crop, 23, 52. *See also* Garlic farming; Lamjaj trees; Peanut farming

Census data, of village households, 21, 22, 52

Central Thai ethic prejudices of, 11; neolocal residence patterns of, 5

Ceremonies: to appease the spirits of the dead, 121, 122; enjoyed by old people, 88–89; to honor ancestral spirits, 117–118; for ordination, 96–97

Charmer, 68; description of, 50; labor of in fields, 54–55; position of in family, xiii

Index

Chiangmai Village, 16; auspicious directions in, 36; average household size in, 52; concept of marriage in, 102–103; cooperation in rice growing enterprises in, 58–60; factionalism in, 83, 89–91; food economy in, 91; identity via work in rice fields in, 58; location of, 23; map of, 26; markets near, 71–73; politics in, 89–91; as a pseudonym, xv, 11; rice land in, 52–54; school in, 50, 84; sexual division of labor in, 56–57; sexual standards in, 11, 108, 117; status of women in, 21; structural conflicts in, 18; temple as symbol of unity in, 83; and youth training project, 70. *See also* Economic life; Family life and structure; Temple; Women

Chiengmai, Thailand, 9; markets of, 71; training center and jobs in, 70

Chiengmai Valley, 23, 25

Childbirth, death from, 30, 33, 120–122

Children: deference of to parents, 102; division of property among, 6, 54; individual economic enterprises of, 60–75; money earned by given to parents, 61–64, 65, 66; terms of address for, 102. *See also* Courtship; Youngest daughter

Chinese daughter-in-law, 20

Chinese traders, 70, 71, 72

Cigarettes, 102

Clothes: of children, 50; and courtship, 104, 111; for ordination ceremony, 96–97; for religious occasions, 84; types of, 76–77; washing and ironing of, 77, 78–79

Coconuts, 73

Comic opera, 89

Compound family group, 10; cycle of, 13–14

Conflicts: crucial structural, 18; women as mediators in, 30, 101

Consanguines: in female-centered system, 20; female spirits of, 115

Conversation patterns, in courtship, 104–108

Courtship, 103–112; conversations of, 104–108; customs of to ease fears, 103–104; distrustfulness in, 103, 105–106, 108, 119; groups of young men for, 104, 111; importance of in family structure, 101; parental interference in, 7, 109–110; standards of sexual behavior in, 108, 117

Courtyard, 23–51; animals in, 49; authority over, 30; buildings in, 49–50; description of, 24, 27, 30; main house in, 30–39, 48–49; money trees from, 94; protective spirits of, 116; social interaction in, 76, 81, 84; visitors to, 27, 30, 50–51

Courtyard land, inheritance of, 53

Cremation, 120

"Crystal child," 96–97; picture of Keen as, 98

Crystal Rise Village, 88

Dairy cows, 70

Dancing, at the temple, 84, 95

Davis, Richard, 16; on ideological dominance of men, 18–19; on ritual matriliny, 18

De Young, John, 5

Death, from childbirth, 32, 33, 120–122

Deceptiveness: fear of, 102, 103, 108, 119; of spirits and in human relationships, 119, 122

Decorations, for the temple, 93–94

Deference: of children to parents, 99, 102; and money earned by children, 61–66 *passim*; of son-in-law, 100. *See also* Senior-junior relationships

Descent groups: and agricultural labor exchange groups, 58–60; matrilineal, 15–18; model of ideal type according to Turton, 16; role of in economic life, 17–18. *See also* Lineality; Matrilineal ancestral spirits

Directions, auspicious, 36

Don Daeng Village, kinship system in, 14–15

Dressmaking school, 69

Drumming contest, 84

Drums, 84, 87

Dust, in houses, 76

Eating habits, 78. *See also* Food preparation; Meals

Economic cooperation: and kinship, 12; structural ties for, 58–60

Index

Ghosts, from death in childbirth, 33, 118, 120‑122
Girls: job specialty of, 68
Golden Lady drum, 84, 87
Gongs, 84, 92
Gossip, and courtship, 103, 108
Government funds, 91
Grandfather Ten Thousand: authority of, 30, 39, 100, 112-113; influence of on Plenitude family, 112-114; opposition of to Moonlight's marriage, 110; and ordination of Keen, 96; position of in family, xv
Grandmother Heart's Content: as mistress of ceremonies for matrilineal spirits, 118; as susceptible to spirit possession, 51
Grandmother Worth: activities of at the temple, 84-85, 88-89; description of, 38; diminished capabilities of and deference to, 102; house inherited by, xv, 53, 116; photograph of, 39; position of in family, xv; spirits near bed of, 38, 115
Greeting, polite words of, 50
Groups: for agricultural labor exchange, 58-60, 90; for courtship, 104; for food donated to the temple, 92-93, 94; as structural ties, 90. *See also* Agricultural labor exchange groups; Matrilineal ancestral spirits; Neighborhood group

Haas, Mary, xv
Hair color, 69
Hairdressing, occupation of, 33, 68-69
Headmen, 66; and village factionalism, 89-91 *passim*
Holy Day, xi; cooking duties of, 76, 77; courtship of, 104, 112; description of, 48; ducks cared for by, 77-78; field work by, 80; money earned by, 64-66; photograph of, 46; position of in family, xiv; as research assistant, 22; water jars filled by, 78
House(s): description of, 23, 30; inheritance of, 54, 116; as "old-established," 116, 117; spirits returning to, 121-122. *See also* Main house

Households, 6, 12; average size of, 52; cycle of compound structures in, 13-14; economic cooperation among, 12, 58-60
Husband: incorporated into wife's spirit cult, 19; in-laws residing with, 19; matriline membership of, 100-101, 116, 117; money of to propitiate wife's matrilineal spirits, 100, 117; status of, 101. *See also* Marriage; Son-in-law

Identity, and work in rice fields, 58
Illness, caused by spirits, 117, 119
Incest rules, 117
Individual family members: activities of at the temple, 84-98; economic enterprises by, 60-75
Inheritance: of authority, 20, 55, 100-101, 123; and division of property among children, 6, 54; father in control of, 6, 7; of houses, 54, 63, 100, 116; of land, 52-54; as not discussed, 22, 54; rules of, 19; of son, 101

Java, matrifocal system in, 21

Kaufman, Howard, 10; on sexual division of labor, 56; on social differences between marriage partners, 7; on typology of family groups, 6-7, 10
Keen: activities of at the temple, 96-98; agricultural work of, 56-57, 78, 80; attitude of Grandfather Ten Thousand toward, 113-114; courtship by, 81, 104, 111-112; economic orientation of, 62; illness of, 119; impact of marriage on, 62, 101; job training and opportunities for, 69-70; photographs of, 33, 45, 96, 98; position of in family, xiv
Kingshill, Konrad, 83; on family structure in Northern Thailand, 5-6
Kinship: bilateral, 14; and economic cooperation, 12, 59; extragenealogical considerations of, 9; of Plenitude family, 27; and residence patterns, 10-11; statistical model of, 9-10; symbolized by membership in spirit cults, 19; as

Index

Medicine show, 81
Meetings at the temple, 84; of the school committee, 89-91; of youth groups, 97-98
Men: dress of, 76-77; formal authority of, 99-101; ritual position of in spirit cults, 17; as superior to women, 15, 99-100. *See also* Authority; Husband; Male affines; Son-in-law
Mîaŋ, 71
Mistress of ceremonies, 117-118
Mizuno, Koichi, on kinship patterns, 14-15
Moerman, Michael, 83; kinship description of, 8-9, 13
Money: earned by children and given to parents, 61-66 *passim*; tree, donated to the temple, 94; unit of, 64
Monks: food donated to, 91, 92; restricted to the temple, 84; and schools, 89. *See also* Novice
Moonlight, xi, 85; activities of at the temple, 94-95; courtship of, 110-111; food preparation by, 77; hairdressing project of, 68-69; ironing clothes by, 78; job of in lamjaj harvest, 66; money earned by, 63; photographs of, 33, 44; position of in family, xiv; as a research assistant, 22
Morality: and dance patterns, 95; tales of, 85, 88. *See also* Sexual behavior
Mother Celestial: activities of at the temple, 91-93; bedroom of, 38; and courtship of her daughters, 109-110; food preparation by, 79; house inherited by, 116; influence of Grandfather Ten Thousand on, 39, 113; marriage of, 38-39, 100, 102-103; morning work of, 76; photograph of, 41; position of in family, xiii, 101; spirits encountered by, 118
Motorcycles, 111
Mulder, J.A. Niels, 11, 12

Names: of characters in Plenitude family, xiii-xv; and matrilineal spirits, 116; and terms of address, 33; of wife after marriage, 19, 100
Neighborhood group: in labor exchange group, 59; as a structural tie, 90

Neolocal nuclear family, 10
Neolocal residence patterns, 5
New Dawn (youngest daughter): childhood of, 102; commands and directions to, 39, 48, 102; courtship of, 104, 112; as a dancer, 95-96; field work of, 80; inheritance of, 54, 63, 100-101; 116; laundry duties of, 77; photograph of, 47; position of in family, xiv; as a research assistant, 22; spirits encountered by, 118
Nodding Rubber Trees, market of, 73
Northern Thailand: anthropological field work in, 5-6, 8-9, 12-22, 123-124; lineality in, 20, 99, 123; traditional garments of, 76-77
Novice: evening meal of, 92; life of, 96-97; and merit for the mother, 17

Old people: activities at the temple for, 84-85, 88-89; diminished capabilities of and deference to, 102; respect for, 38, 88, 102; socializing of, 85
Older Brother Eye, 88, 90; as dominated by father-in-law, 54-55; position of in family, xiii, 50
Older Sister Blessing: activities of at the temple, 93-94; description of, 38; economic orientation of, 61-62; individual enterprises by, 65-66; market activities of, 73-76, 79; marriage of, 62, 110; photograph of, 43; position of in the family, xiii
Older Sister Clear: description of, 50; market activities of, 73-75, 76, 79; marriage of, 50, 109; photograph of, 42; position of in family, xiii
Older Sister Fine Qualities: death of in childbirth, 30, 33, 120-122; marriage of, 109; position of in family, xiv; spirit of, 118, 120-122
Older Sister Valuable, 51, 81
Orchard Grove, market at, 71-73
Ordination, reason for and ceremony of, 96-97

Parents: care of in old age, 54, 116, 102; and courtship of children, 109-110; and educational training of children,

134

of older family members, 102; as principle in family social structure, 99, 100. *See also* Respect

Sexual behavior, 11; during courtship, 108; and matrilineal spirits, 117

Sexual division of labor, 56–57

Sharp, Lauriston: on sexual division of labor, 56; on Thai family structure, 5, 7

Sleeping mats, 38

Smith, Harvey, on Thai family structure, 10–11

Social organization: for economic cooperation, 58–60; and political allies, 90–91; and ritual, 13; structural ties in, 90, 99, 123–124

Social relationships in the family, 99–114; basic principles of, 99–100, 123–124; power of women in, 101, 103; spirits as indicative of, 115. *See also* Authority; Courtship; Lineality; Matrilineal ancestral spirits

Socializing: in the evening, 81; of old people at the temple, 85

Solien de Gonzales, Nancie, 21

Son-in-law: avoidance taboo of, 50, 55, 101; burdens of role of, 112–113; deference of, 100; dominated by father-in-law, 55; and spirit possession, 15

Spin Out Gold: description of, 38; engagement and courtship of, 63–64, 109; money earned by, 63–64, 66; part-time job of, 70, 80; photograph of, 45; piglets raised by, 66–67; portage of rice to mill by, 78, 79; position of in family, xiv

Spirit cults: associated with matrilineal descent, 15–18, 90; membership in, 19. *See also* Matrilineal ancestral spirits

Spirit medium, 121

Spirit possession: personality susceptible to, 51; and son-in-law, 15

Spirits, 115–122; appeasing of, 119–120, 121; in deceptive forms, 118–119; and delimiting a kin group, 10; kinds of, 115; as malevolent and deceiving, 118–119; of people who died unfulfilled, 120–122; as reflecting human relationships and characteristics, 119, 122; re-

turn of to house, 121–122. *See also* Matrilineal ancestral spirits

Surnames, 100

"Take a day, return a day" system, 58, 65

Tambiah, S.J., 4, 14, 83; on auspicious directions, 36*n*; diachronic analysis of, 13–14; structural perspective of, 12–13

Taxis: and malevolent spirits, 120; for transportation to the markets, 74–76

Tea leaves, fermented, 71

Teakwood Crest Village, 52, 53

Temple: activities for old people provided by, 84–85, 88–89; dancers of, 95; decorations for, 93–94; donations to on behalf of the dead, 121; and family life, 83–98; food donated to, 91–93, 94; formality of, 94–95; meetings at, 84, 89, 97–98; ordination of a novice at, 96–97; range of activities provided by, 84–98; school committee of, 89–90; as a social context for family members, 84; as setting for village politics, 89–91, 98

"Tender soul," and spirit possession, 51

Thai-German Dairy, 69–70

Thai-Yuan descent group, 15–16, 17

Thailand: king and queen of, 30; previous anthropological research about, 2–19. *See also* Loose structure theory

Tobacco, selling of, 71

Turton, Andrew: contribution of, 18; on family relationships, 17; on matrilineal descent groups, 15–18; on role of descent groups in economic life, 17–18

Uxorilocality, 10

Village: ideal of help in, 58; levels of organization in, 16; proverbs in, 118–119; spirit dance in, 51; youth group in, 69. *See also* Chiangmai Village; Headmen

Visiting, 30, 81

Wage, average, 70

Water buffalo meat, 80–81, 93

Printed in the United States
42718LVS00002B/22-84